The Psalms • Part II

OneBook.

DAILY–WEEKLY

The Psalms · Part II

Brian D. Russell

Printed in the United States of America

Cover design by Strange Last Name
Page design by PerfecType, Nashville, Tennessee

Russell, Brian D., 1969-
The Psalms. Part II / Brian D. Russell. – Frankin, Tennessee : Seedbed Publishing, ©2017.

x, 100 pages ; 21 cm. + 1 videodisc – (OneBook. Daily-weekly)

ISBN 9781628244373 (paperback)
ISBN 9781628244410 (DVD)
ISBN 9781628244380 (Mobi)
ISBN 9781628244397 (ePub)
ISBN 9781628244403 (uPDF)

1. Bible. Psalms -- Textbooks. 2. Bible. Psalms -- Study and teaching.
3. Bible. Psalms -- Commentaries. I. Title. II. Series.

BS1430.55 .R872 2017 223/.206 2016907761

SEEDBED PUBLISHING
Franklin, Tennessee
seedbed.com

CONTENTS

WELCOME TO ONEBOOK DAILY-WEEKLY

John Wesley, in a letter to one of his leaders, penned the following:

> O begin! Fix some part of every day for private exercises. You may acquire the taste which you have not: what is tedious at first, will afterwards be pleasant. Whether you like it or not, read and pray daily. It is for your life; there is no other way; else you will be a trifler all your days. . . . Do justice to your own soul; give it time and means to grow. Do not starve yourself any longer. Take up your cross and be a Christian altogether.

Rarely are our lives most shaped by our biggest ambitions and highest aspirations. Rather, our lives are most shaped, for better or for worse, by those small things we do every single day.

At Seedbed, our biggest ambition and highest aspiration is to resource the followers of Jesus to become lovers and doers of the Word of God every single day, to become people of One Book.

To that end, we have created the OneBook Daily-Weekly. First, it's important to understand what this is not: warm, fuzzy, sentimental devotions. If you engage the Daily-Weekly for any length of time, you will learn the Word of God. You will grow profoundly in your love for God, and you will become a passionate lover of people.

How does the Daily-Weekly work?

Daily. As the name implies, every day invites a short but substantive engagement with the Bible. Five days a week you will read a passage of Scripture followed by a short segment of teaching and closing with a question for reflection and self-examination. On the sixth day, you will review and reflect on the previous five days.

Weekly. Each week, on the seventh day, find a way to gather with at least one other person doing the study. Pursue the weekly guidance for gathering. Share learning, insight, encouragement, and most important, how the Holy Spirit is working in your lives.

That's it. Depending on the length of the study, when the eight or twelve weeks are done, we will be ready with the next study. On an ongoing basis we will release new editions of the Daily-Weekly. Over time, those who pursue this course of learning will develop a rich library of Bible learning resources for the long haul.

OneBook Daily-Weekly will develop eight- and twelve-week studies that cover the entire Old and New Testaments. Seedbed will publish new studies regularly so that an ongoing supply of group lessons will be available. All titles will remain accessible, which means they can be used in any order that fits your needs or the needs of your group.

If you are looking for a substantive study to learn Scripture through a steadfast method, look no further.

WEEK ONE

Book II: Finding Hope in the Psalms of Korah

ONE

Welcome to Books II and III of the Psalter

Key Observation. Books II and III of Psalms point us away from human rulers to focus on trust in the Lord alone.

Understanding the Word. Welcome to our journey through Book II (Pss. 42–72) and Book III (Pss. 73–89). Books II and III of Psalms serve a key function within the whole. In OneBook Daily-Weekly *The Psalms—Part I,* we observed the overall movement of the book by beginning with a study of the Psalter's introduction (Pss. 1–2) and conclusion (Pss. 146–150). The Psalter opens by grounding God's people in faithfulness through meditation on Scripture (Ps. 1) and ultimate security through God's reign over the nations through the Messiah (Ps. 2). The Psalter's climax (146–150) is a celebration of God's victory in which all creation joins together to praise the Lord.

In Psalms 3–145, life happens. The Psalter serves as our prayer book as God's missional people. God calls us to live as his hands, feet, and mouthpieces in the world. As people seeking to embody the gospel, we are God's witnesses to a world that does not yet know or worship the Lord. Given this reality, life brings challenges. Sometimes these challenges are our own doing because of unfaithfulness. Other times, God's people find themselves in seasons of chaos through the evil intentions of enemies, bouts with illness, or catastrophic events. In all circumstances, the book of Psalms awaits our careful reading. As

Scripture, its words give us a voice to praise the Lord and to cry out for God's salvation. Through the Psalter's pages we will encounter a language of faith that can sustain us in our journey.

In Book I, we encountered a mix of cries for help (laments); anchoring psalms that reminded God's people of the importance of Scripture and instruction (Torah psalms); rich praises for who God is (praise); expressions of gratitude for answers to prayer (thanksgiving); hymns about God's Messiah (royal psalms); and affirmations of deep trust (psalms of trust).

Books II and III reveal that the final compilers of the Psalms showed careful thought in how they arranged the whole. If Book I mostly contains psalms bearing a heading that includes the phrase "Of David," it is striking that Books II and III introduce two new phrases in their headings: "Of Asaph" and "Of the Sons of Korah." Asaph and Korah were both important Levitical priests, and their families served as singers and liturgists in the temple. If we step back and just observe these headings, we find that Books II and III are organized by them. Notice how the blocks of psalms linked to Korah and Asaph form bookends around the central block of Davidic material in Psalms 51–72 and Psalm 86:

Psalms 42–49: Korah
Psalm 50: Asaph
Psalms 51–72: David
Psalms 73–83: Asaph
Psalms 84–85: Korah
Psalm 86: David
Psalms 87–88: Korah

This places the focus in these books on Israel's trust in God's reign through King David and his descendants. Yet we will find that this trust created a crisis of faith. In the Davidic psalms, the king was under constant stress. Moreover, in Book III, there will be a national crisis of faith in light of the exile to Babylon. These psalms will invite God's people to find security in God alone.

1. Reflect on your life. In whom or in what do you find true security?

2. What is your present sense of your journey of faith in Jesus?

TWO

Psalm 42

Psalm 42 (ESV) *As a deer pants for flowing streams, so pants my soul for you, O God. 2My soul thirsts for God, for the living God. When shall I come and appear before God? 3My tears have been my food day and night, while they say to me all the day long, "Where is your God?" 4These things I remember, as I pour out my soul: how I would go with the throng and lead them in procession to the house of God with glad shouts and songs of praise, a multitude keeping festival.*

5Why are you cast down, O my soul, and why are you in turmoil within me? Hope in God; for I shall again praise him, my salvation 6and my God. My soul is cast down within me; therefore I remember you from the land of Jordan and of Hermon, from Mount Mizar. 7Deep calls to deep at the roar of your waterfalls; all your breakers and your waves have gone over me. 8By day the L*ORD* *commands his steadfast love, and at night his song is with me, a prayer to the God of my life. 9I say to God, my rock: "Why have you forgotten me? Why do I go mourning because of the oppression of the enemy?" 10As with a deadly wound in my bones, my adversaries taunt me, while they say to me all the day long, "Where is your God?"*

11Why are you cast down, O my soul, and why are you in turmoil within me? Hope in God; for I shall again praise him, my salvation and my God.

Key Observation. Putting our hope in the living God is foundational for the life of faith.

Understanding the Word. Book II of the Psalter opens with a psalm rich in meaning. It captures the essence of the faith that we will discover in Psalms 42–89. It begins with the image of a thirsty deer longing for cool waters of a pristine stream. The psalmist likened this to his soul's desire for a fresh encounter with God. Psalms 42 and 43 highlight a conversation between the psalmist and his soul.

The psalmist referred to "soul" throughout the prayer (vv. 1, 2, 4–6, and 11). It is important to understand the meaning of the Hebrew word *nephesh* that is translated "soul." Too often we equate soul with the spiritual part of ourselves that is separate from our physical body. This is a misunderstanding of the biblical concept. When the psalmist talked about soul, he was talking about the whole of himself as a living, breathing person. When the psalmist said, "My soul thirsts for God" (42:2), he was saying that all aspects of his being (mental, physical, spiritual, and emotional) are desperate for God. His words expressed a desire to connect fully with God. He felt separated from God and longed for a time to be in God's presence.

The psalmist was desperate for God because of taunts from unnamed enemies (v. 3) and because of memories of worship (v. 4). The psalmist recalled moments at the temple when God's people celebrated the protective care of the Lord. In other words, the psalmist longed for the communal worship of God and the feelings of security that God provides. The absence of this caused the psalmist's grief and trouble.

In verse 5, we find the chorus that recurs three times within Psalm 42 (vv. 5 and 11) and Psalm 43 (v. 5)—"Why are you cast down, O my soul?" In response to his distress, the psalmist questioned his despair and encouraged himself to place hope in God. This will be a key reminder for God's people. There will be difficult times personally and communally. But there remains one source of hope: the living God. In the Old Testament, God's people remembered the God of the exodus; in the New Testament, God's people focus on the life, death, and resurrection of Jesus. The psalmist built on his hope in the Lord by anticipating future opportunities to praise God for his salvation. A consistent theme in the Psalter is the ability for God's people to praise God even in the midst of difficult circumstance.

Verses 6–10 provide more details about the psalmist's plight and prayer. He was geographically far from Jerusalem (v. 6). The mighty roar of the headwaters of the Jordan River reminded the psalmist of his smallness and frailty in the world (v. 7). In response, he confessed his knowledge of God's ongoing love as well as his recognition that God is the source and grounding of his life (v. 8). On the basis of this relationship, the psalmist cried out to God to act on his behalf against his foes (vv. 9–10).

Psalm 42:11 ends the prayer with the same refrain as in verse 5.

1. What do you desire most in the world? How is this desire similar to or different from the psalmist's longing for God?

2. What is your most meaningful worship experience? How did it shape you?

THREE

Psalm 43

Psalm 43 *Vindicate me, my God, and plead my cause against an unfaithful nation. Rescue me from those who are deceitful and wicked.* [2]*You are God my stronghold. Why have you rejected me? Why must I go about mourning, oppressed by the enemy?* [3]*Send me your light and your faithful care, let them lead me; let them bring me to your holy mountain, to the place where you dwell.* [4]*Then I will go to the altar of God, to God, my joy and my delight. I will praise you with the lyre, O God, my God.*

[5]*Why, my soul, are you downcast? Why so disturbed within me? Put your hope in God, for I will yet praise him, my Savior and my God.*

Key Observation. We respond to God's grace with praise and worship.

Understanding the Word. Based on the repetition of a common refrain (42:5, 11, and 43:5), it appears that Psalms 42 and 43 were originally one psalm. Psalm 43 completes the lament begun in Psalm 42. If Psalm 42 focused on the psalmist's plight, Psalm 43 centers on the psalmist's cry for help. In Psalm 42, we learned that the psalmist was under the oppression of enemies far from the temple and longed to praise God in the temple with fellow believers.

The psalmist's lament was bold and daring. Verse 1 is the language of the courtroom. The psalmist asked God to make a summary judgment by affirming his innocence. The psalmist recognized two realities. First, he asserted his innocence. This is a common theme in the Psalms, but can sound arrogant or even naive to our twenty-first-century ears. Second, the psalmist was resolute that God could and *should* save him. Thus, he begged God to do so.

In verse 2, the psalmist confessed that God is his *stronghold* (or, *refuge* in the ESV). This is the grounding for the psalmist's confidence and hope. But

God does not seem to be living up to his reputation. Why does it seem as though God has rejected the psalmist and left him oppressed and mourning in the presence of enemies?

The heart of the psalmist is evident in verses 3–4. Obviously the psalmist desired deliverance. But note the purpose of the deliverance. He desired to praise God with the faithful. Therefore, the psalmist called on God to send illumination and faithfulness as guides through the present darkness. First John will later affirm that "God is light" (1:5) and "God is love" (4:8). These are reminders for us as we journey through the world. Regardless of the challenges and the present darkness we may face, God's core essence remains light and love.

The purpose of the psalmist's pleadings was to gain him the opportunity to worship God in Jerusalem. The psalmist demonstrated a pious desire to worship God in the place that the Lord chose—Jerusalem. This was a key theme in Psalm 42 as well. Psalms 42–43 hold a high opinion of regular and enthusiastic worship of God by his people. Verse 4 serves both as an indication of the purpose of the psalmist's deliverance and also a promise by the psalmist to respond to God's grace and salvation with praise and worship. This is a core value and model for us. God acts—we give thanks and worship.

Psalm 43 ends with the psalmist's self-talk (see 42:5, 11) to remain dialed into God.

1. What kind of person do we have to become to be able to plead our innocence before God with integrity?
2. What role does worship play in the psalmist's desire for God?

FOUR

Psalm 44

Psalm 44 *We have heard it with our ears, O God; our ancestors have told us what you did in their days, in days long ago.* [2]*With your hand you drove out the nations and planted our ancestors; you crushed the peoples and made our ancestors flourish.* [3]*It was not by their sword that they won the land, nor did their arm* *bring them victory; it was your right hand, your arm, and the light of your face, for you loved them.*

4You are my King and my God, who decrees victories for Jacob. 5Through you we push back our enemies; through your name we trample our foes. 6I put no trust in my bow, my sword does not bring me victory; 7but you give us victory over our enemies, you put our adversaries to shame. 8In God we make our boast all day long, and we will praise your name forever.

9But now you have rejected and humbled us; you no longer go out with our armies. 10You made us retreat before the enemy, and our adversaries have plundered us. 11You gave us up to be devoured like sheep and have scattered us among the nations. 12You sold your people for a pittance, gaining nothing from their sale.

13You have made us a reproach to our neighbors, the scorn and derision of those around us. 14You have made us a byword among the nations; the peoples shake their heads at us. 15I live in disgrace all day long, and my face is covered with shame 16at the taunts of those who reproach and revile me, because of the enemy, who is bent on revenge.

17All this came upon us, though we had not forgotten you; we had not been false to your covenant. 18Our hearts had not turned back; our feet had not strayed from your path. 19But you crushed us and made us a haunt for jackals; you covered us over with deep darkness.

20If we had forgotten the name of our God or spread out our hands to a foreign god, 21would not God have discovered it, since he knows the secrets of the heart? 22Yet for your sake we face death all day long; we are considered as sheep to be slaughtered.

23Awake, Lord! Why do you sleep? Rouse yourself! Do not reject us forever. 24Why do you hide your face and forget our misery and oppression?

25We are brought down to the dust; our bodies cling to the ground. 26Rise up and help us; rescue us because of your unfailing love.

Key Observation. During difficult seasons, God's people must pray confidently to the God who has shown his grace and mercy in the past.

Understanding the Word. Psalm 44 is a prayer for help by the entire community. "We" is the subject of many of the lines in this prayer. Communal psalms will become more common as we move deeper into the Psalter. As we will soon see, Books II and III of the Psalter begin to focus on a national crisis facing God's people. Book II opens with two related individual cries for help to God. Psalm 44 moves us beyond the individual to a cry for help by the entire community. Psalm 44 includes a mix of historical reflection on what God has done in the past (vv. 1–8), confusion over God's inaction in the present (vv. 9–16), the pleading of the innocence of God's people in keeping covenant (vv. 17–22), and a final plea for help (vv. 23–26).

The psalm opens with the community remembering God's gracious acts of salvation in the past (vv. 1–8). Specifically for God's people in the Old Testament, this meant reflection on the exodus from Egypt and the gift of the land of Canaan (vv. 1–2). The psalmist emphasized that these were the actions of God alone (vv. 3–8). God gifted Israel all of the blessings enjoyed by the people of God. Likewise as followers of Jesus, we focus on his life, death, and resurrection as the foundation for our relationship and identity as God's missional people. These opening lines remind us that we are recipients of God's kindness and love. How do we respond to God's graciousness? With praise and thanksgiving (v. 8).

Our psalm takes a surprising turn in verses 9–16. Despite God's past graciousness, God's people are presently experiencing humiliation and defeat. Verse 11 is powerful: "You gave us up to be devoured like sheep and have scattered us among the nations." God's people suffered the taunting of enemies. In the ancient world, one of the most potent taunts was, "Where is your god?" The enemies of Israel believed that their ability to defeat God's people showed the Lord's weakness and ineffectiveness. This heightened the misery of God's people.

In verses 17–22, God's people pled their innocence. They had practiced faithfulness and not forgotten their covenant relationship with the Lord (v. 17). They had carefully kept their hearts clean and in tune with God (vv. 18–21). God's people asserted their innocence both in their external actions and in their thoughts. How then could they be suffering at the hands of their enemies (v. 22)?

As we live together as God's missional people, we may well face seasons corporately when the world seems against us and God appears absent or unconcerned. Have you ever been there? How do we pray in such times?

Verses 23–26 model a poignant prayer of desperation for God. God has acted in the past. God's love is real and is the final force in history. Therefore, even when all may seem lost, we pray confidently to the One who can save us.

1. Reflect on your community of faith's history with God. How does God's past work within your congregation serve to encourage you today?
2. How does Psalm 44 serve as a model for praying as a community to God during difficult seasons?

FIVE

Psalm 45

Psalm 45 *My heart is stirred by a noble theme as I recite my verses for the king; my tongue is the pen of a skillful writer.*

2You are the most excellent of men and your lips have been anointed with grace, since God has blessed you forever.

3Gird your sword on your side, you mighty one; clothe yourself with splendor and majesty. 4In your majesty ride forth victoriously in the cause of truth, humility and justice; let your right hand achieve awesome deeds. 5Let your sharp arrows pierce the hearts of the king's enemies; let the nations fall beneath your feet. 6Your throne, O God, will last for ever and ever; a scepter of justice will be the scepter of your kingdom. 7You love righteousness and hate wickedness; therefore God, your God, has set you above your companions by anointing you with the oil of joy. 8All your robes are fragrant with myrrh and aloes and cassia; from palaces adorned with ivory the music of the strings makes you glad. 9Daughters of kings are among your honored women; at your right hand is the royal bride in gold of Ophir.

10Listen, daughter, and pay careful attention: Forget your people and your father's house. 11Let the king be enthralled by your beauty; honor him, for he is your lord. 12The city of Tyre will come with a gift, people of wealth will seek your favor. 13All glorious is the princess within her chamber; her gown is interwoven with gold. 14In embroidered garments she is led to the king; her virgin companions follow her—those brought to be with her. [15]*Led in with joy and gladness, they enter the palace of the king.*

[16]*Your sons will take the place of your fathers; you will make them princes throughout the land.*

[17]*I will perpetuate your memory through all generations; therefore the nations will praise you for ever and ever.*

Key Observation. Israel's Davidic king modeled holiness and led God's mission in the world.

Understanding the Word. Psalm 45 is a hymn of praise for the wedding of Israel's king. It celebrates kingship. In the Psalter, songs about the king serve as reminders of security. The king functioned as God's agent for administering and leading God's kingdom. The king was God's anointed one (or messiah). Royal songs also serve as symbols of hope. As Christians, we read the royal psalms in the knowledge that Jesus fulfills the longings of these prayers.

Verse 1 gives us direct insight about the psalm's author. One of the sons of Korah enjoyed the honor of composing a psalm in the king's honor. This psalm flows out of the psalmist's being. As we cultivate praise, gratitude, and prayer through faithful practice, we are able to experience these as a natural outflow of our connection with God.

The remainder of the psalm divides into two sections: verses 2–6 and 7–16, with verse 17 serving as a conclusion. These two sections are blessings over the king in two areas: his power to rule over God's kingdom and his ability to reproduce sons who will rule after him. These two themes flow out of God's promises to David in 2 Samuel 7:8–16. Israel's hope is, in part, centered on God's establishment of David and his descendants as the rulers for God's people.

In verses 2–6, the psalmist prayed a word of blessing over the power of the king. First, the psalmist praised the king for his appearance. The king appeared in the splendor of battle gear. But the key attribute is not appearance or pure power, but mission. All ancient kingdoms boasted about their kings' power. This psalm celebrates God's victories through the king, but notice the language of verse 4. The king modeled virtues that demonstrate God's holiness: truth, humility, and justice. Israel's messiah led God's mission. This was not about defeating enemies for exploitation and conquest, but to defend the mission of God's people to bless the nations by spreading the knowledge of God (see Genesis 12:3; Exodus 19:4–6; cf. 1 Samuel 17:46). It is vital to remember that God was not for his people *against* the nations but for his people *for the sake* of the nations.

Second, verse 6 celebrates the eternal security of God's throne and Davidic rule. In Psalm 89, there is a lament over the loss of Davidic rule during exile (see Week 8), but in the long view of God's work, it is truth. Jesus embodies and fulfills this vision (see Hebrews 1:8).

The second half of the Psalm (vv. 7–16) celebrates the king's marriage and sons whom the queen will bear. This speaks of Israel's historic kings. As Christians, we read this as a symbol for Jesus' work "in bringing many sons and daughters to glory" (Heb. 2:10).

Verse 17 is a fitting climax. Generations of God's people will remember the king, and the nations will praise him. This envisions the fulfillment of God's mission to bless the nations and foreshadows the Psalter's vision for praise by all living beings (see Psalm 150:6).

1. How is Israel's vision of its king different from typical understandings of kingship?
2. How does Jesus fulfill Psalm 45's words?

WEEK ONE

GATHERING DISCUSSION OUTLINE

A. Open session in prayer.

B. View video for this week's reading.

C. What general impressions and thoughts do you have after considering the video and reading the daily writings on these Scriptures? What, specifically, did this week's psalms teach you about faith, life, and prayer?

D. Discuss selected questions from the daily readings. Always invite class members to share key insights or to raise questions that they found to be the most meaningful.

1. **KEY OBSERVATION:** Books II and III of the Psalms point us away from human rulers to focus on trust in the Lord alone.

   DISCUSSION QUESTION: Reflect on your life. In whom or in what do you find true security?

2. **KEY OBSERVATION (PSALM 42):** Putting our hope in the living God is foundational for the life of faith.

   DISCUSSION QUESTION: What do you desire most in the world? How is this desire similar to or different from the psalmist's longing for God?

3. **KEY OBSERVATION (PSALM 43):** We respond to God's grace with praise and worship.

DISCUSSION QUESTION: What role does worship play in the psalmist's desire for God?

4. **KEY OBSERVATION (PSALM 44):** During difficult seasons, God's people must pray confidently to the God who has shown his grace and mercy in the past.

   DISCUSSION QUESTION: Reflect on your community of faith's history with God. How does God's past work within your congregation serve to encourage you today?

5. **KEY OBSERVATION (PSALM 45):** Israel's Davidic king modeled holiness and led God's mission in the world.

   DISCUSSION QUESTION: How is Israel's vision of its king different from typical understandings of kingship?

E. Close session with prayer.

WEEK TWO

Book II: Finding Security in the Psalms of Korah and Asaph

ONE

Psalm 46

Psalm 46 (ESV) *God is our refuge and strength, a very present help in trouble.*
[2]Therefore we will not fear though the earth gives way, though the mountains be
moved into the heart of the sea, [3]though its waters roar and foam, though the
mountains tremble at its swelling. Selah

[4]There is a river whose streams make glad the city of God, the holy habitation
of the Most High. [5]God is in the midst of her; she shall not be moved; God will
help her when morning dawns. [6]The nations rage, the kingdoms totter; he utters
his voice, the earth melts. [7]The Lord of hosts is with us; the God of Jacob is our
fortress. Selah

[8]Come, behold the works of the Lord, how he has brought desolations on the
earth. [9]He makes wars cease to the end of the earth; he breaks the bow and shat-
ters the spear; he burns the chariots with fire. [10]"Be still, and know that I am God.
I will be exalted among the nations, I will be exalted in the earth!" [11]The Lord of
hosts is with us; the God of Jacob is our fortress. Selah

Key Observation. Calmness and security are found in relationship with the true King of creation—the Lord.

Understanding the Word. Psalms 46–48 form a trio of psalms that envision a secure foundation for the life of faith. They focus us as God's people on the key relationship that guarantees our future. Each psalm serves as a praise to the Lord as the true King of the earth.

Psalm 46 opens with a bold confession. Our God is present always as a refuge in times of trouble. Chew on that for a few minutes. God is not wishy-washy. God is not only a God of the good times. The psalmist reminds us that God is dependable and present even in crisis moments when all seems lost.

Verses 2–3 draw out the full implications of God-given security. We can lay aside our deepest fears. We all fear something. The psalmist, however, refused to fear even the undoing of creation. Verses 2–3 describe a scenario in which creation (earth, mountains, sea, and waters) disintegrates. He pictured the catastrophic end of the world. The psalmist proclaimed that with God there is always a future *no matter what comes*. That is true security.

The psalm takes a dramatic shift in verses 4–7. Its focus turns to the security and calm of God's city: Jerusalem. In the Old Testament, Jerusalem or Zion represented the center of God's kingdom. In Jerusalem stood the two pillars of God's presence: the Davidic king (or messiah) and the temple, where the glory of the Lord inhabited. Jerusalem was the city of the great King, who reigned through his messiah and whom the people worshiped in the temple. These verses describe peace in the midst of the chaos and uproar of the nations. The kingdoms of this world may threaten and practice violent injustice, but the true King is a fortress for his people who find refuge in him.

So what does the refuge of God mean for God's people in a world of chaos and insecurity? This is an important question for us in the twenty-first century, as our world is no less chaotic than it was in the psalmist's day.

In verses 8–11, God speaks directly to creation, including all of the raging nations. It is a portrait of the future kingdom of God, when God makes all things new. These verses invite everyone (including the raging nations) to come and catch a glimpse of God's abundant and peaceful future. Verse 10 brings Psalm 46 to a memorable climax with its call to stillness in the midst of the chaos of the present. There is a way to peace and security. It is not war. It is not manifestations of power and rage. Peace and security come from *knowing* and *experiencing* God as the exalted Lord and true King. The Lord is our refuge. We can live faithfully as his hands, feet, and mouthpieces in the world because the Lord has secured the future.

1. Reflect on your deepest fears. How does Psalm 46 invite you to overcome them?

2. How often do you take time to quiet your mind and reflect on the greatness of God? Where in your present life can you carve out five to ten minutes to create a daily practice?

TWO

Psalm 47

Psalm 47 *Clap your hands, all you nations; shout to God with cries of joy.*

[2]For the Lord Most High is awesome, the great King over all the earth. [3]He subdued nations under us, peoples under our feet. [4]He chose our inheritance for us, the pride of Jacob, whom he loved.

[5]God has ascended amid shouts of joy, the Lord amid the sounding of trumpets. [6]Sing praises to God, sing praises; sing praises to our King, sing praises. [7]For God is the King of all the earth; sing to him a psalm of praise.

[8]God reigns over the nations; God is seated on his holy throne. [9]The nobles of the nations assemble as the people of the God of Abraham, for the kings of the earth belong to God; he is greatly exalted.

Key Observation. Psalm 47 models an unbridled praise for the living God, who reigns and desires to bless all.

Understanding the Word. Following the confident language of Psalm 46, Psalm 47 begins with exuberance.

The praise of God's people in Psalms 46–48 is bold and daring for its context. In the Old Testament, Israel was not a significant nation militarily or politically. The larger and more menacing foes in Egypt or Mesopotamia (the Assyrians and Babylonians) always threatened Israel. Yet God's people steadfastly believed that their God, the Lord, was the true King over all the earth. To proclaim the Lord as King was a declaration that he was greater than all of the other gods worshiped around the globe. Psalm 47 leads us in praise but also helps us understand the significance of praising God as King. This is a vital word for the twenty-first century. Sometimes we may find ourselves discouraged by the day's events or the decline of values around us. Yet, like the psalmist, we can raise our voices in the praise of the Lord.

Verse 1 opens with a general call for all peoples and nations to recognize and honor the Lord for who he is. This psalm imagines the day when all the earth will worship the Lord. The book of Psalms anticipates a future where "everything that has breath praise[s] the LORD" (Ps. 150:6, author's paraphrase). At this point of our journey through the Psalter, Psalm 47 serves to encourage God's people because they do not yet see a universal desire to praise God.

In verses 2–4, Israel testified to the nations about the Lord. God is the true King because of his awesomeness on behalf of God's people. Verses 3–4 retell God's victories in giving God's people their land, and in particular their "[heritage] pride of Jacob," that is, Jerusalem, where God's temple stands.

In verses 5–7 God is a victorious warrior marching to claim his throne. These verses call for praise as the Lord passes by. For his victories, Psalm 47 declares again that the Lord is King of all the earth (vv. 2, 7, and 8). How are we to respond to the King of all the earth? With praise and worship.

Verses 8–9 describe God's global reign. Peace abides, and all peoples gather for worship. In verse 9, the psalmist described the nations as "the people of the God of Abraham." This is significant. Abraham marked the beginning of God's people. God gave Abraham a mission. Abraham was to serve as the agent of blessing to all nations (see Genesis 12:3). This is a reminder of the missional significance of our witness. God's people exist to testify to the world of the greatness of God and the wideness of his grace.

As followers of Jesus, we worship and serve the crucified and risen Lord Jesus, who will someday be universally worshiped as Lord (see Philippians 2:9–11). As we long for that day, Psalm 47 encourages us to keep on praising.

1. How, specifically, does Psalm 47 teach us to praise the Lord?
2. What is the significance of praising the Lord as the King of all of the earth?

THREE
Psalm 48

Psalm 48 *Great is the LORD, and most worthy of praise, in the city of our God, his holy mountain.*

2Beautiful in its loftiness, the joy of the whole earth, like the heights of Zaphon is Mount Zion, the city of the Great King. 3God is in her citadels; he has shown himself to be her fortress.

4When the kings joined forces, when they advanced together, 5they saw her and were astounded; they fled in terror. 6Trembling seized them there, pain like that of a woman in labor. 7You destroyed them like ships of Tarshish shattered by an east wind.

8As we have heard, so we have seen in the city of the LORD Almighty, in the city of our God: God makes her secure forever.

9Within your temple, O God, we meditate on your unfailing love. 10Like your name, O God, your praise reaches to the ends of the earth; your right hand is filled with righteousness. 11Mount Zion rejoices, the villages of Judah are glad because of your judgments.

12Walk about Zion, go around her, count her towers, 13consider well her ramparts, view her citadels, that you may tell of them to the next generation.

14For this God is our God for ever and ever; he will be our guide even to the end.

Key Observation. When we understand our security in God, we are able to witness, testify, and take actions to spread the good news to others.

Understanding the Word. Psalm 48 proclaims daringly that God controls the future. God's kingdom will be the final word in history. Psalm 48 invites us to anticipate God's decisive victory over all forces of darkness and evil. Until that day, God's people live with the certainty that the future is secure regardless of the temporary challenges of the present.

Verses 1–3 rehearse many of the same themes that we've read this week in Psalms 46–47. The psalmist praised God for his greatness and for providing security for his people from his holy city, Zion. This is a portrait of Zion/Jerusalem as God's holy mountain. The language of verse 2 is common in the ancient world. The ancients associated gods with mountains. For example, the Greeks linked Zeus to Mount Olympus. The Canaanites believed that Baal ruled from Mount Zaphon. By claiming the superiority and beauty of Zion over Zaphon, the psalmist declared that the Lord alone is the true King and God over the earth. As followers of Jesus, we recognize that God is no longer associated with a single place of worship. The temple in Jerusalem has been replaced with the body of Christ. However, when we pray Psalm 48, we gain a sense of security in the present and hope for the future, when Jesus will reign forever in a kingdom centered on a New Jerusalem (see Revelation 21:2).

In verses 4–8, the psalmist envisioned the nations coming against Zion in force (cf. Psalm 2:1–3). But after one look at God's city and mountain, they quake, cower, and run for cover (vv. 6–7). God's people celebrate this victory in the eternal security of God's city (v. 8).

God's people respond to their secure surroundings with adoration for their great God. At the core of their reflection on God's actions are memories of God's loyal and faithful love (v. 9). The Lord is a protector and a king, but unlike others gods, at the center of God's character is a committed love. God's love fuels his mission in the world. The psalm moves from a security centered on Zion/Jerusalem to a vision of God's name sweeping across the earth (v. 10). This is a reminder for God's people that God is not for his people *against* the nations, but *for the sake* of the nations. God's victories for his people are part of his mission to bless all nations (see Genesis 12:3). When we understand our security in God, we are able to witness, testify, and take actions to spread the good news to others.

Psalm 48 concludes (vv. 12–14) with praise for God by God's people. Likewise, the psalmist exhorts God's people to share their experiences of God with the next generation because God's guidance, love, and security will endure forever. Amen.

1. How, specifically, does Psalm 48 describe the future hope of God's people?
2. How does our assurance of security in God help serve as a basis for participating in God's mission in the present?

FOUR
Psalm 49

Psalm 49 (ESV) *Hear this, all peoples! Give ear, all inhabitants of the world, [2]both low and high, rich and poor together! [3]My mouth shall speak wisdom; the meditation of my heart shall be understanding. [4]I will incline my ear to a proverb; I will solve my riddle to the music of the lyre.*

[5]Why should I fear in times of trouble, when the iniquity of those who cheat me surrounds me, [6]those who trust in their wealth and boast of the abundance of their riches? [7]Truly no man can ransom another, or give to God the price of his life, [8]for the ransom of their life is costly and can never suffice, [9]that he should live on forever and never see the pit.

[10]For he sees that even the wise die; the fool and the stupid alike must perish and leave their wealth to others. [11]Their graves are their homes forever, their dwelling places to all generations, though they called lands by their own names. [12]Man in his pomp will not remain; he is like the beasts that perish.

[13]This is the path of those who have foolish confidence; yet after them people approve of their boasts. Selah [14]Like sheep they are appointed for Sheol; death shall be their shepherd, and the upright shall rule over them in the morning. Their form shall be consumed in Sheol, with no place to dwell. [15]But God will ransom my soul from the power of Sheol, for he will receive me. Selah

[16]Be not afraid when a man becomes rich, when the glory of his house increases. [17]For when he dies he will carry nothing away; his glory will not go down after him. [18]For though, while he lives, he counts himself blessed—and though you get praise when you do well for yourself—[19]his soul will go to the generation of his fathers, who will never again see light. [20]Man in his pomp yet without understanding is like the beasts that perish.

Key Observation. Beware of relying on wealth and riches for one's eternal security.

Understanding the Word. Psalm 49 develops the theme of security in God (Psalms 46–48) by reflecting on a practical question. Psalm 49 wants to teach a vital lesson to those who pray it. It warns against the folly in trusting in wealth for security in this life. The temptation of finding personal security in wealth is one common to all people everywhere—including people of faith. We may profess our trust in God, but we put a great deal of faith in our wallets. Let's reflect on the words of the psalmist.

Verses 1–4 establish the wisdom of the psalm as beneficial for "all inhabitants of the world." The Lord is King of the earth, so God's truth is for all people. The teaching of Psalm 49 applies for rich or poor.

The instruction of Psalm 49 is clear. It is folly to put one's trust in wealth and riches. Only God is worthy of our trust. The psalmist was not pandering to those who lack material goods. All people need enough resources to provide for basic necessities—food, clothing, and shelter. Scripture does not glorify the poor, nor does it vilify the rich. Psalm 49 serves as a direct reminder that wealth is only an asset during this life. Verses 5–9 reflect on this truth. The psalmist refused to fear difficult times and pushed away the temptation to join the rich in putting their trust in their own resources (vv. 5–6). This is folly because it is short-sighted. This psalm does not deny that money can provide comfort (v. 18), but it is insistent that this is a foolish solution because it is only short-term. The reality is that no amount of wealth can buy life in the next age. The psalmist insisted that we take a broader view of life and death.

Verses 10–15 remind us that *everyone* dies—wise and foolish alike. We can eat right, exercise, and amass huge retirement accounts, but one day our earthly existence will end. The issue is whether we will live wisely or foolishly. What is the key distinction between the wise and foolish? It is not the size of one's bank account or number of one's possessions. The only relationship that determines one's future is our relationship with God. Verse 15 contains astonishing news. The psalmist shared a deep confidence that God will ransom his soul from Sheol, that is, the grave! This is the hope of life after this life. The wise person cultivates a relationship with God, and it lasts for all eternity.

Verses 16–20 end with a renewed warning about trusting riches. Wealth provides some comfort, but it can be a fool's gold because it does not guarantee the future—only a moment-by-moment walk with God does. As followers of Jesus, we remember our Lord's words: "But seek first his kingdom and his righteousness, and all these things [our basic necessities] will be given to you as well" (Matt. 6:33).

1. Why do you think that the Bible warns so much against trusting in wealth?

2. Assess your relationship with wealth. (Be honest.) Does your present security depend more on God or on your acquired wealth?

FIVE

Psalm 50

Psalm 50 *The Mighty One, God, the Lord, speaks and summons the earth from the rising of the sun to where it sets. [2]From Zion, perfect in beauty, God shines forth. [3]Our God comes and will not be silent; a fire devours before him, and around him a tempest rages. [4]He summons the heavens above, and the earth, that he may judge his people: [5]"Gather to me this consecrated people, who made a covenant with me by sacrifice." [6]And the heavens proclaim his righteousness, for he is a God of justice.*

[7]"Listen, my people, and I will speak; I will testify against you, Israel: I am God, your God. [8]I bring no charges against you concerning your sacrifices or concerning your burnt offerings, which are ever before me. [9]I have no need of a bull from your stall or of goats from your pens, [10]for every animal of the forest is mine, and the cattle on a thousand hills. [11]I know every bird in the mountains, and the insects in the fields are mine. [12]If I were hungry I would not tell you, for the world is mine, and all that is in it. [13]Do I eat the flesh of bulls or drink the blood of goats?

[14]"Sacrifice thank offerings to God, fulfill your vows to the Most High, [15]and call on me in the day of trouble; I will deliver you, and you will honor me."

[16]But to the wicked person, God says:

"What right have you to recite my laws or take my covenant on your lips? [17]You hate my instruction and cast my words behind you. [18]When you see a thief, you join with him; you throw in your lot with adulterers. [19]You use your mouth for evil and harness your tongue to deceit. [20]You sit and testify against your brother and slander your own mother's son. [21]When you did these things and I kept silent, you thought I was exactly like you. But I now arraign you and set my accusations before you.

[22]"Consider this, you who forget God, or I will tear you to pieces, with no one to rescue you: [23]Those who sacrifice thank offerings honor me, and to the blameless I will show my salvation."

Key Observation. Living faithfully with gratitude and love for neighbor is more important than only practicing formal religious acts.

Understanding the Word. Psalms 42–49 arose from the Korahites. Psalm 50 connects with the Asaphites. Korah and Asaph were Levitical priests during the reign of David. Beginning in Psalm 51 we will encounter a block of psalms associated with David (51–72), including a single psalm with the heading "Of Solomon" (72), which ends with the words, "This concludes the prayers of David son of Jesse" (v. 20), before moving back to psalms associated with Asaph and Korah.

Book II of the Psalms (Psalms 42–72) focuses on practicing faithful obedience in the full confidence and security of God. This does not keep God's people immune from difficult times, but it points to the need to keep faith in all circumstances. God can be trusted.

Psalm 50 is a worthy way to end our week of study. It serves as both an exhortation and a warning. It builds on the themes of Psalms 46–48 regarding the security that God's people have in the God of Zion.

In verses 1–6, God calls to all the earth from Zion. Psalm 50 envisions final judgment. God has the future under control and is the sole judge. He appears in triumph and power. Just as on Mount Sinai, the Lord is surrounded by fire and wind (see Exodus 19:16–19). Verse 1 addresses God as "Mighty One, God, the Lord." Psalm 50 divides between the faithful and the wicked. This stark division is reminiscent of Jesus' parable of the sheep and goats (see Matthew 25:31–46).

In verses 7–15, God warns against trusting in sacrifice over relationship. God's people have been faithful in offering animals, but God reminds them that *all creatures* already belong to him (vv. 10–11). God does not need to be fed (vv. 12–13). Instead, he desires an authentic sacrifice of thanksgiving and an honoring of vows (v. 14). It is vital for us to reflect on this. God does not desire our *rote* obedience. He desires our hearts and minds. God values a thank you over an obligation. When we make a promise to God, he desires us to keep it. Practicing a ritual-based religion is insufficient. Verse 15 reminds us that God desires our prayers in times of trouble. God will deliver us so that we may witness to his greatness. Thanksgiving and prayer form the foundation for an authentic relationship with God.

In the last section of the psalm (vv. 16–23), God warns against unfaithfulness. He accuses the wicked of breaking many of the Ten Commandments (see Exodus 20:1–17). These are breaches of relationship with others. The Scriptures call for us to love God and neighbor. The wicked focus on external religious acts, such as animal sacrifice, apart from living mercifully and justly in relationship with others.

Verse 23 describes the way of the righteous, who will experience full salvation. It is not about outward religious acts. In fact, to rely on only external actions is to forget God and experience judgment. What does God desire from his people? Worship offered to the Lord with a spirit of gratitude and thanksgiving.

1. Why do you think the psalmist warns against relying on formal religious acts?
2. In what ways do you practice thanksgiving and gratitude in your current life? Give some examples.

WEEK TWO

GATHERING DISCUSSION OUTLINE

A. Open session in prayer.

B. View video for this week's reading.

C. What general impressions and thoughts do you have after considering the video and reading the daily writings on these Scriptures? What, specifically, did this week's psalms teach you about faith, life, and prayer?

D. Discuss selected questions from the daily readings. Always invite class members to share key insights or to raise questions that they found to be the most meaningful.

1. **KEY OBSERVATION (PSALM 46):** Calmness and security are found in relationship with the true King of creation—the Lord.

   DISCUSSION QUESTION: Reflect on your deepest fears. How does Psalm 46 invite you to overcome them?

2. **KEY OBSERVATION (PSALM 47):** Psalm 47 models an unbridled praise for the living God, who reigns and desires to bless all.

   DISCUSSION QUESTION: How, specifically, does Psalm 47 teach us to praise the Lord?

3. **KEY OBSERVATION (PSALM 48):** When we understand our security in God, we are able to witness, testify, and take actions to spread the good news to others.

DISCUSSION QUESTION: How does our assurance of security in God help serve as a basis for participating in God's mission in the present?

4. **KEY OBSERVATION (PSALM 49):** Beware of relying on wealth and riches for one's eternal security.

   DISCUSSION QUESTION: Assess your relationship with wealth. (Be honest.) Does your present security depend more on God or on your acquired wealth?

5. **KEY OBSERVATION (PSALM 50):** Living faithfully with gratitude and love for neighbor is more important than only practicing formal religious acts.

   DISCUSSION QUESTION: Why do you think the psalmist warns against relying on formal religious acts?

E. Close session with prayer.

WEEK THREE

Book II: Psalms of David (Prayers for the Valley, Part I)

ONE

Psalm 51:1–2

Psalm 51:1–2 (ESV) *Have mercy on me, O God, according to your steadfast love; according to your abundant mercy blot out my transgressions.* [2]*Wash me thoroughly from my iniquity, and cleanse me from my sin!*

Key Observation. "If we confess our sins, he is faithful and just to forgive us our sins and purify us from all unrighteousness" (1 John 1:9).

Understanding the Word. Psalms 51–72 offer a Davidic core at the heart of Books II–III. Most of the psalms include "Of David" or are untitled except for Psalm 72 ("Of Solomon"). Psalm 72 concludes with, "This concludes the prayers of David son of Jesse" (v. 20). Moreover, eight of these psalms (Psalms 51, 52, 54, 56, 57, 59, 60, and 63) include references to challenges in David's life from the books of Samuel in their headings. By linking psalms to difficult episodes in David's life, the psalms remind us that even godly kings such as David still faced challenging seasons. As we seek to live out God's mission in the world, we must recognize that this commitment will not translate into a worry-free or stormless life. For the next two weeks, we will explore these Davidic prayers as models for our own during times of need.

We begin with one of the most well-known psalms from Book II: Psalm 51. This psalm is a penitential prayer (prayer for forgiveness). The others are Psalms 6, 32, 38, 102, 130, and 143.

Psalm 51 is a model prayer of repentance, sorrow, restoration, and renewal. In 2 Samuel 11–12, David sinned greatly but turned wholeheartedly to the Lord. Israel's great king committed adultery with a woman named Bathsheba. Then, after Bathsheba became pregnant with David's child, he ordered her husband, Uriah, murdered. The words in Psalm 51 attempt to capture the spirit of his prayer as a model for all God's people on how to pray when we have sinned. It serves as a reminder of the grave burden and consequences of sin, but also of the great mercy of God.

God desires for us to walk faithfully in love of God and neighbor, but when we do sin, God invites us to pray. As Jesus' followers, we have this promise: "If we confess our sins, he is faithful and just and will forgive us our sins and purify us from all unrighteousness" (1 John 1:9).

The psalmist cut to the heart of the matter in verses 1–2. There are no excuses, justifications, or nuances in the psalmist's words. He opened immediately with a request for God's mercy and grace. The psalmist could pray boldly because he knew God's character. He based his request on God's faithful love and abundant compassion. These are God's core characteristics. The psalmist recognized his guilt and uncleanness before God. God was his only hope. Verse 2 imagines sin and transgression as a filthy contamination that needs to be cleansed in the same way that dirty clothes must be washed.

The opening verses of Psalm 51 may remind readers of the prayer of the tax collector in Luke 18:13: "God, have mercy on me, a sinner." This was a prayer that Jesus affirmed as one that God answers. So it will be with those who pray Psalm 51.

1. How do verses 1–2 teach us about praying to God for forgiveness?
2. What are areas in your life for which you need to ask for God's mercy and grace?

TWO

Psalm 51:3–19

Psalm 51:3–19 (ESV) *For I know my transgressions, and my sin is ever before me.* [4]*Against you, you only, have I sinned and done what is evil in your sight, so* *that you may be justified in your words and blameless in your judgment. [5]Behold, I was brought forth in iniquity, and in sin did my mother conceive me. [6]Behold, you delight in truth in the inward being, and you teach me wisdom in the secret heart.*

[7]Purge me with hyssop, and I shall be clean; wash me, and I shall be whiter than snow. [8]Let me hear joy and gladness; let the bones that you have broken rejoice. [9]Hide your face from my sins, and blot out all my iniquities. [10]Create in me a clean heart, O God, and renew a right spirit within me. [11]Cast me not away from your presence, and take not your Holy Spirit from me. [12]Restore to me the joy of your salvation, and uphold me with a willing spirit.

[13]Then I will teach transgressors your ways, and sinners will return to you. [14]Deliver me from bloodguiltiness, O God, O God of my salvation, and my tongue will sing aloud of your righteousness. [15]O Lord, open my lips, and my mouth will declare your praise. [16]For you will not delight in sacrifice, or I would give it; you will not be pleased with a burnt offering. [17]The sacrifices of God are a broken spirit; a broken and contrite heart, O God, you will not despise.

[18]Do good to Zion in your good pleasure; build up the walls of Jerusalem; [19]then will you delight in right sacrifices, in burnt offerings and whole burnt offerings; then bulls will be offered on your altar.

Key Observation. God desires to cleanse us deeply and profoundly from sin by restoring us so that we can turn outward for the good of the world.

Understanding the Word. Yesterday we began with the first two verses of Psalm 51. The psalmist's remaining prayer breaks up into three sections: verses 3–8, 9–17, and 18–19.

Verses 3–5 summarize the psalmist's sorrow. There are no excuses—just confession of guilt. The psalmist did not attempt to hide wrongdoing, but admitted that his transgressions are ever-present burdens (v. 3). Moreover, he recognized that these sins were against God. Yes, when we sin, we hurt others and ourselves, but our sins are ultimately against our loving Creator (v. 4). It is to God we will answer. The psalmist ended this section with a categorical confession of lostness (v. 5). His recent failures were recurring patterns. He had been trapped in sinful cycles since conception. The psalmist recognized his inability to save himself. There was only one solution: the mercy, grace, and unfailing love of God. Often God's greatest work begins on the ruin of our lives when we turn to him fully.

In verses 6–8, the psalmist again requested cleansing. He continued his view of his sinfulness as a stain that needed removed (cf. v. 2). The psalmist recognized that his inner life did not line up with the expectations and will of God (v. 6). He asked for God's cleansing (v. 7) so that he could return to a life of joy and fulfillment. Sin will weary us. We must be sensitive to our need for God's grace and turn to the Lord whenever we stray from God's ways.

Verses 9–17 focus on specifics for renewal and include vows of actions that the restored psalmist will take. Verses 9–12 lyrically capture the heart and passion of this prayer. The link to David is powerful. The great king had sinned and the stakes were sky-high. David threw himself fully into the arms of God, knowing that *only* God could restore him. He wanted his sins and iniquity removed (v. 9), but more important, he wanted his moment-by-moment relationship with God to be healed (vv. 10–12). This required a work beginning in his inner core—his heart. In Hebrew, "heart" refers to a person's thinking and decision-making center.

In verses 13–17, the psalmist vowed to teach others the way of the Lord and to confess publicly the praise of God. Experiences of God's grace must always be spread and shared with others. Moreover, verse 17 reminds us of the posture with which we must approach God. Confession must be authentic. The psalmist was shattered by his sin. He approached God not with sacrifices, but by freely admitting brokenness and lostness.

Psalm 51 concludes with a prayer that moves beyond the sorrowful psalmist to include blessings for Jerusalem/Zion (vv. 18–19). This is a reminder that our prayers must move beyond ourselves. Sin is subtle. It continually attempts to guide us into a deeper sense of individual entitlement and self-centered focus. The mark of the truly repentant, in part, is the ability to pray beyond our personal needs for the good of the community around us.

1. How, specifically, does Psalm 51 teach you to pray when you have sinned?

2. Describe how the psalmist understood restoration, renewal, and forgiveness.

THREE
Psalm 52

Psalm 52 (ESV) *Why do you boast of evil, O mighty man? The steadfast love of God endures all the day. [2]Your tongue plots destruction, like a sharp razor, you worker of deceit. [3]You love evil more than good, and lying more than speaking what is right. Selah [4]You love all words that devour, O deceitful tongue.*

[5]But God will break you down forever; he will snatch and tear you from your tent; he will uproot you from the land of the living. Selah [6]The righteous shall see and fear, and shall laugh at him, saying, [7]"See the man who would not make God his refuge, but trusted in the abundance of his riches and sought refuge in his own destruction!"

[8]But I am like a green olive tree in the house of God. I trust in the steadfast love of God forever and ever. [9]I will thank you forever, because you have done it. I will wait for your name, for it is good, in the presence of the godly.

Key Observation. We must respond to evil with gratitude and trust in the assurance of God's good future.

Understanding the Word. Like Psalm 51, Psalm 52 connects its content with a specific episode in David's life. It is another difficult time, but unlike Psalm 51, where David's sin brought calamity upon him, Psalm 52 is a prayer when David suffered due to the evil actions of others. The heading of Psalm 52 refers to the actions of Doeg the Edomite in 1 Samuel 21–22. In these chapters, David was fleeing for his life from King Saul. He stopped at a shrine to the Lord at Nob where the priest Ahimelech served. Ahimelech aided David without knowing that David was a fugitive, but Doeg witnessed this and informed Saul. Saul ordered Doeg to execute Ahimelech and his family. This serves as the inspiration for Psalm 52 and invites us to consider circumstances in life when well-intentioned actions are repaid with evil.

Psalm 52 laments times when godly people suffer at the hands of those with evil and self-serving intentions. These are times when life seems unfair. In our minds, godly living ought to lead to positive outcomes. Yet, in practice, we often experience the opposite. Scripture warns us, "Indeed, all who desire to live a godly life in Christ Jesus will be persecuted" (2 Tim. 3:12 ESV). How do we pray in such times? Psalm 52 guides us.

In verses 1–4, the psalmist denounced the unjust and evil actions of an arrogant oppressor. Verse 1a addresses the evildoer as "O mighty man." This is language typically used to describe a hero. But this person is no hero. He has acted against the godly and boasts in it. The person is proud that he has put one over on the people of God. Verse 1b stands in contrast by reminding us that God's loyal and steadfast love lasts forever. Evil may have its day, but God's ways are eternal.

The psalmist then described the motives behind evil action. Verse 3 is powerful, "You love evil more than good." The result of this motivation is a tongue that creates chaos for the godly.

The way of the wicked will come to an end (see Psalm 1:6). Verses 4–7 envision a day when God will make all things right. Evil may bear fruit for a time, but God will bring a reversal. Justice is the hope of God's people. It will come.

Psalm 52 ends with the psalmist taking the posture of a person fully committed to the ways of the Lord regardless of present outcomes (vv. 8–9). Unlike the boastful evildoer, the psalmist was calm and steady like an olive tree in God's garden (v. 8). The psalmist responded with trust in God's steady and loyal love that lasts forever. God's love is the final word in human history. We prepare for this future by standing in it today with trust (v. 8) and thanksgiving (v. 9). This posture of gratitude and trust serves as a testimony to God's goodness. Perhaps such a witness will also invite evildoers to a better way of living.

1. How does this prayer teach us to pray and live during times when others falsely accuse and persecute us?
2. How, specifically, did the psalmist act and find hope in response to the evil actions of others?

FOUR

Psalm 53

Psalm 53 *The fool says in his heart, "There is no God." They are corrupt, and their ways are vile; there is no one who does good.*

[2]*God looks down from heaven on all mankind to see if there are any who understand, any who seek God.* [3]*Everyone has turned away, all have become corrupt; there is no one who does good, not even one.*

[4]*Do all these evildoers know nothing?*

They devour my people as though eating bread; they never call on God. [5]*But there they are, overwhelmed with dread, where there was nothing to dread. God scattered the bones of those who attacked you; you put them to shame, for God despised them.*

[6]*Oh, that salvation for Israel would come out of Zion! When God restores his people, let Jacob rejoice and Israel be glad!*

Key Observation. The wise trust in God's justice and security despite the chaos caused by fools.

Understanding the Word. In Psalm 52, we reflected on the damage that a person intent on evil can do in the short term. Psalm 53 reflects deeply on the inner workings of an evildoer. Psalm 53 is almost identical to Psalm 14. This repetition emphasizes the importance of the reflection on human wickedness and its causes. As God's missional people, who seek to share God's blessings with others, we face the perplexing issue of the ongoing capacity for people to act against God's loving desires for the world.

Evil rarely makes sense. Psalm 53 reflects on it and sees it as the logical result of folly. In the book of Psalms as well as in Proverbs, there is often a contrast between the wise and the fool. These categories are not about intellectual level or education. They are about how one relates to God. The wise person's life finds its grounding in a reverent fear and respect for the Lord (see Proverbs 1:7). As we will see, the fool lives as if there were no God. Thus, Psalm 53 offers a warning to outsiders to embrace the ways of God. Likewise, it warns God's people who are trying to model love for God and neighbor of the irrational nature of human sinfulness. God's people must live wisely (see Ephesians 5:15).

Psalm 53 views human corruption as the natural result of a heart issue. Remember that "heart" refers to the will, intentions, and thinking center of a person. Thus, at the core of his or her being, the fool denies the activity and existence of the true Creator and King of the universe. This denial is a fatal flaw. In Matthew 15:19, Jesus made a similar observation: "For out of the heart come evil thoughts—murder, adultery, sexual immorality, theft, false testimony, slander."

Verses 1b–3 describe the characteristics of fools and the outflow of their hearts. They act in corrupt ways and model evil (v. 1b). So many follow this pattern that the psalmist imagined God looking down from the heavens on humanity in an attempt to find wise people who seek to love God and neighbor. According to verse 3, he found no one. Paul cited this text in his reflection on human lostness apart from God's grace through Jesus (see Romans 3:11).

Yet the psalmist affirmed the existence of the godly (vv. 4–6). They are victims of the foolish. The psalmist, who knew God, did not understand the foolish (v. 4). So he focused on the long view (v. 5). There is no hope in a life lived apart from God. Fools may enjoy practicing evil, oppression, and injustice for a season, but their end is certain, and it will not be a positive outcome, as God is just.

The psalmist ended with a plea that God would indeed act *now* to restore the fortunes and joy of God's people. This is a prayer for us during times when all hell has broken loose and we feel surrounded on all sides by ill-intentioned people.

1. What are the marks of a foolish person? Of a wise person?
2. How does Psalm 53 invite you to live your life as a witness to true wisdom?

FIVE

Psalm 54

Psalm 54 (ESV) *O God, save me by your name, and vindicate me by your might. [2]O God, hear my prayer; give ear to the words of my mouth.*

[3]For strangers have risen against me; ruthless men seek my life; they do not set God before themselves. Selah

[4]Behold, God is my helper; the Lord is the upholder of my life. [5]He will return the evil to my enemies; in your faithfulness put an end to them.

[6]With a freewill offering I will sacrifice to you; I will give thanks to your name, O LORD, for it is good. [7]For he has delivered me from every trouble, and my eye has looked in triumph on my enemies.

Key Observation. When surrounded by enemies, we must relinquish our need to control and, instead, find help and refuge in the God who is able to save us.

Understanding the Word. This week we've focused on the enemy *within* (our capacity for sin and its results) and *without* (the ongoing presence of evildoers who threaten God's people). The book of Psalms offers a rich reading of the potentials and pitfalls of life as we seek to follow Jesus on mission into the world. Through connections with episodes in King David's life, the Davidic psalms remind us that the life of faith does not insulate us from difficulties arising from our flaws or from the ill intentions of others. In all circumstances, the Psalms point us to the living God as the source for hope, security, and peace. Psalm 54 continues this thread.

The heading for Psalm 54 refers to a story in 1 Samuel 23:15–29, where David was hiding from Saul in the wilderness of Ziph. Some of Ziph's residents reported this to Saul and placed David in danger. Psalm 54 is a lament that cries out to God for salvation from one's foes. It teaches us how to pray when enemies afflict us.

The psalmist cried out directly to God (vv. 1–2). He needed God to hear his prayer and save him. The psalmist appealed to God's name for help. In the Old Testament, a person's name embodied his essence and power. The psalmist was in extreme distress and recognized that God's power alone could save him. We can imagine the fear and dread that David felt when the location of his hideout became public. There will be times in our lives when we lose control of our safety and fear for our futures. There is only one place to turn—the Lord.

The psalmist was in extreme danger (v. 3). His life was at risk. The people afflicting him did not play by the rules, did not follow the ways of God, and intended only evil.

The psalmist responded by clinging desperately to God (v. 4). There was no attempt to scheme or plot an escape. Survival depended on someone or something outside the psalmist's control. The psalmist affirmed his faith and trust in the Lord as his helper and the One who supported and sustained him.

The psalmist specifically asked God to put an end to his enemies. This may seem harsh and even unchristian, but recognize this: the psalmist was expressing deep human emotion. He knew that his life might well end and that his only hope was the removal of his foes. The key here is that the psalmist *relinquished* final judgment and action to God. This was not a prayer for personal vengeance. He trusted God to take the proper and just action.

Verses 6–7 conclude with a vow to offer sacrifices and praise on the other side of this challenge. The psalmist showed confidence that God is faithful in delivering God's people from harm because the Lord is good. When we are recipients of God's gracious mercies, our role is to testify to God's greatness.

1. Describe the confidence of the one praying this psalm.
2. What kind of person does Psalm 54 assume that we are so that we can pray its words with integrity?

WEEK THREE

GATHERING DISCUSSION OUTLINE

A. Open session in prayer.

B. View video for this week's reading.

C. What general impressions and thoughts do you have after considering the video and reading the daily writings on these Scriptures? What, specifically, did this week's psalms teach you about faith, life, and prayer?

D. Discuss selected questions from the daily readings. Always invite class members to share key insights or to raise questions that they found to be the most meaningful.

1. **KEY OBSERVATION (PSALM 51:1–2):** "If we confess our sins, he is faithful and just and will forgive us our sins and purify us from all unrighteousness" (1 John 1:9).

   DISCUSSION QUESTION: How do verses 1–2 teach us about praying to God for forgiveness?

2. **KEY OBSERVATION (PSALM 51:3–19):** God desires to cleanse us deeply and profoundly from sin by restoring us so that we can turn outward for the good of the world.

   DISCUSSION QUESTION: Describe how the psalmist understood restoration, renewal, and forgiveness.

3. **KEY OBSERVATION (PSALM 52):** We must respond to evil with gratitude and trust in the assurance of God's good future.

DISCUSSION QUESTION: How does this prayer teach us to pray and live during times when others falsely accuse and persecute us?

4. **KEY OBSERVATION (PSALM 53):** The wise trust in God's justice and security despite the chaos caused by fools.

   DISCUSSION QUESTION: What are the marks of a foolish person? Of a wise person?

5. **KEY OBSERVATION (PSALM 54):** When surrounded by enemies, we must relinquish our need to control and, instead, find help and refuge in the God who is able to save us.

   DISCUSSION QUESTION: What kind of person does Psalm 54 assume that we are so that we can pray its words with integrity?

E. Close session with prayer.

WEEK FOUR

Book II: Psalms of David (Prayers for the Valley, Part II)

ONE

Psalm 55

Psalm 55 *Listen to my prayer, O God, do not ignore my plea; [2]hear me and answer me. My thoughts trouble me and I am distraught [3]because of what my enemy is saying, because of the threats of the wicked; for they bring down suffering on me and assail me in their anger.*

[4]My heart is in anguish within me; the terrors of death have fallen on me. [5]Fear and trembling have beset me; horror has overwhelmed me. [6]I said, "Oh, that I had the wings of a dove! I would fly away and be at rest. [7]I would flee far away and stay in the desert; [8]I would hurry to my place of shelter, far from the tempest and storm."

[9]Lord, confuse the wicked, confound their words, for I see violence and strife in the city. [10]Day and night they prowl about on its walls; malice and abuse are within it. [11]Destructive forces are at work in the city; threats and lies never leave its streets.

[12]If an enemy were insulting me, I could endure it; if a foe were rising against me, I could hide. [13]But it is you, a man like myself, my companion, my close friend, [14]with whom I once enjoyed sweet fellowship at the house of God, as we walked about among the worshipers.

[15]Let death take my enemies by surprise; let them go down alive to the realm of the dead, for evil finds lodging among them.

[16]As for me, I call to God, and the LORD saves me. [17]Evening, morning and noon I cry out in distress, and he hears my voice. [18]He rescues me unharmed from the battle waged against me, even though many oppose me. [19]God, who

is enthroned from of old, who does not change—he will hear them and humble them, because they have no fear of God.

[20]My companion attacks his friends; he violates his covenant. [21]His talk is smooth as butter, yet war is in his heart; his words are more soothing than oil, yet they are drawn swords.

[22]Cast your cares on the LORD and he will sustain you; he will never let the righteous be shaken. [23]But you, God, will bring down the wicked into the pit of decay; the bloodthirsty and deceitful will not live out half their days.

But as for me, I trust in you.

Key Observation. When we find ourselves in times of trial, we must release all of our concerns and feelings to the God whom we can trust.

Understanding the Word. All five of this week's psalms are laments associated with David. Living out God's mission as his people means experiencing heartrending challenges and crises. Faith does not immunize us against hardship. But it does give us rich resources for those times when we are walking through valleys.

Psalm 55 is a prayer of an individual who suffered betrayal by a friend. Pain caused by a loved one is soul sapping. Yet the depths of suffering in Psalm 55 are matched by the profound words of the psalmist's prayer.

In verses 1–3, the psalmist cried out to God. The psalmist was in trouble and recognized that only God could help him. The heart of prayer is the recognition of ultimate dependence on God (cf. Matthew 5:3–6).

Verses 4–11 describe the desperation of the situation. The psalmist was surrounded by enemies. He suffered terror. Violence filled the city. He asked God to act. He was trapped. His only hope was God.

What was the situation that the psalmist faced? In verses 12–15, we discover that the psalmist's enemy was actually *a friend.* David suffered the gut-wrenching realization that his pain came from within his community. This cut deep. The anguish of the psalmist's pain increased as he remembered past times of fellowship with this person. But at that moment he needed to ask God to take action against his former companion.

How should we respond to betrayal? Crimes of passion often happen in such circumstances. The psalmist did not take matters into his own hands. Instead, he released the right of retaliation to God. Verses 16–19 model a humble turning to the Lord in prayer for help. The psalmist trusted God to save him. Verse 17 describes the ongoing activity of prayer and invites us to imagine a life lived in moment-by-moment conversation with God (see 1 Thessalonians 5:17). The psalmist recognized God's strength, willingness to hear prayer, and history of acting for good. God would save the psalmist because the enemy refused to know God.

The psalmist returned to his pain (vv. 20–21). Betrayal hurts. When we find ourselves on the end of suffering, we must take it to God. We do not have to sugarcoat anguish. God does not expect us to say, "It's all good!" when its not. Part of learning to pray this psalm is the realization that prayer must be honest. This is for our good; otherwise, we repress feelings that will harm us in the long run. Release your pain to God.

The psalm ends memorably in verses 22–23. The psalmist invites us to bring all of our suffering and cares to the God who will sustain us regardless of circumstances. This is the testimony of the church through the ages. The future is secure. Evil will not prevail. We can bank on it, or as the psalmist said, "I will trust in you" (ESV).

1. Reflect on your ability to be 100-percent honest about your feelings and circumstances with God. Is this difficult or easy for you? Why or why not?
2. What are the characteristics and traits of a person who can pray Psalm 55 with integrity?

TWO

Psalm 56

Psalm 56 (ESV) *Be gracious to me, O God, for man tramples on me; all day long an attacker oppresses me; [2]my enemies trample on me all day long, for many attack me proudly. [3]When I am afraid, I put my trust in you. [4]In God, whose word I praise, in God I trust; I shall not be afraid. What can flesh do to me?*

[5]All day long they injure my cause; all their thoughts are against me for evil. [6]They stir up strife, they lurk; they watch my steps, as they have waited for my life. [7]For their crime will they escape? In wrath cast down the peoples, O God!

[8]You have kept count of my tossings; put my tears in your bottle. Are they not in your book? [9]Then my enemies will turn back in the day when I call. This I know, that God is for me. [10]In God, whose word I praise, in the LORD, whose word I praise, [11]in God I trust; I shall not be afraid. What can man do to me?

[12]I must perform my vows to you, O God; I will render thank offerings to you. [13]For you have delivered my soul from death, yes, my feet from falling, that I may walk before God in the light of life.

Key Observation. Trust rooted in gratitude releases us from fear and opens us to God's work.

Understanding the Word. The heading for Psalm 56 associates it with David's flight to the Philistine city of Gath (see 1 Samuel 21:10–15). He was fleeing King Saul. This was an act of desperation because David was a fearsome enemy of the Philistines, and Gath was the hometown of the giant Goliath, whom David had slain (see 1 Samuel 17). This helps us imagine times in our lives when we have nowhere to run and nowhere to hide. Former friends have become foes, and enemy territory seems safer than our homeland. How do we pray in such times? Psalm 56 shows the way. David's struggles remind God's people of the hardships the godly face in this world.

When we face overwhelming circumstances, we need grace. The psalmist asked God to extend kindness and favor to him (vv. 1–2). Nothing else would pull the psalmist out of his plight. The opening verses stress the grave nature of the psalmist's life. Enemies surrounded him and threatened to trample him.

The psalmist then introduced a refrain focusing on trust (vv. 3–4). It will occur again in verses 10–11. Despite the psalmist's distress, he trusted God. He had experienced fear. Fear can paralyze us. It can erase our confidence. But the psalmist steadfastly declared that he trusted God and, therefore, he refused to be afraid. It is critical to remember that there is only one thing or Being worthy of our fear—God. Scripture says, "Fear of the LORD is the beginning of wisdom" (Ps. 111:10). When we truly fear God, we can be free from the fear of all other people and things because God is the One who guarantees our future. The good news is that the only Being that we should fear is the God who loves us. God demonstrated his love for us by becoming human in Jesus and dying so that we may truly live. This is the God whom the psalmist knew. Therefore, he did not fear.

In verses 5–7, the psalmist described his specific plight. His enemies desired his harm. Yet the psalmist cried out to God for help. Verses 8–10 record the psalmist's confidence that despite his circumstances, he would prevail with God's help.

Verses 10–11 mirror the refrain of verses 3–4. Notice the psalmist's response to danger and fear. He praised the Lord and trusted that God had his best interests at heart. This produced confidence and allowed the psalmist to recognize that he was safe in God's hands.

Verses 12–13 conclude the prayer with a confident glance to a future when the psalmist would give a public thanksgiving to God. We come to God in desperate need with empty hands. God hears us. Then we give thanks and testify to others of his goodness.

1. Make a list of your deepest fears. How does this psalm help you overcome them?
2. What role does gratitude, thanksgiving, and praise serve in this psalm?

THREE

Psalm 57

Psalm 57 *Have mercy on me, my God, have mercy on me, for in you I take refuge. I will take refuge in the shadow of your wings until the disaster has passed.*

[2]*I cry out to God Most High, to God, who vindicates me.* [3]*He sends from heaven and saves me, rebuking those who hotly pursue me—God sends forth his love and his faithfulness.*

[4]*I am in the midst of lions; I am forced to dwell among ravenous beasts—men whose teeth are spears and arrows, whose tongues are sharp swords.*

[5]*Be exalted, O God, above the heavens; let your glory be over all the earth.*

[6]*They spread a net for my feet—I was bowed down in distress. They dug a pit in my path—but they have fallen into it themselves.*

[7]*My heart, O God, is steadfast, my heart is steadfast; I will sing and make music.* [8]*Awake, my soul! Awake, harp and lyre! I will awaken the dawn.*

[9]I will praise you, Lord, among the nations; I will sing of you among the peoples. [10]For great is your love, reaching to the heavens; your faithfulness reaches to the skies.

[11]Be exalted, O God, above the heavens; let your glory be over all the earth.

Key Observation. Times of lament serve as opportunities to grow in our relationship with God through our praise of God's protection.

Understanding the Word. Psalm 57 teaches us how to live courageously under persecution. The heading links us again to a time when David was fleeing from Saul. David faced ongoing injustice as Saul pursued him. God had rejected Saul as king due to his unfaithfulness. David was the anointed one. David refused to take the kingdom by force. Yet Saul attempted to kill him. David's life encourages us. Despite the depths of his anguish, these psalms teach us how to pray and praise God in all circumstances. In his suffering, David foreshadows the Son of David, Jesus the Messiah, who suffered greatly on the cross.

Psalm 57 finds the psalmist in serious trouble. But the psalmist found hope by praising God in exalted language. The lament opens in verse 1. Although our English translation is "Have mercy on me," verse 1 is actually identical to "Be gracious to me" from Psalm 56:1 (ESV). The psalmist recognized his desperate need for God's mercy and grace to save him. The psalmist found in God a "refuge" (cf. Psalm 46:1). This type of prayer indicates to us that the psalmist was all in with God. There was no other help. The reference to "shadow of your wings" refers symbolically to the temple, where the wings of two angelic figures covered the ark of the covenant in the Most Holy Place. The temple in Zion was a place of security. Under the protection of God, the psalmist intended to ride out the storm in which he had found himself.

We see the confidence of the psalmist's prayer in verses 2–3. He referred to God in lofty terms as "Most High." God was both close enough to shadow the psalmist yet simultaneously exalted. This is the biblical portrait of the Lord. He was present yet reigned on high. The psalmist anticipated deliverance from the heavens. Although his enemies sought to trample him, the psalmist knew that God's love and faithfulness would be the final word.

Verses 4–6 describe the psalmist's plight. Enemies described as raging beasts and dangerous hunters surrounded him. Yet God, in his greatness and exhalation, contrasted with these enemies in verse 5 (cf. v. 11). The psalmist was in good hands.

Psalm 57 is an unusual lament. It is full of lofty praise for God. In many ways, the praise drowns out the lament. This is an important word. The psalmist was in grave danger, yet he responded by vigorously lifting up the name of the Lord. The psalm ends beautifully with praise and thanksgiving in verses 7–11. There is no fear in these words. The psalmist affirmed his steadfast trust (v. 7). He roused himself to praise (v. 8). He vowed to praise and give thanks audibly to the world (v. 9). Acts of salvation provide opportunities to testify to the world of God's greatness. The psalmist was confident because of God's steadfast love and faithfulness (v. 10, cf. Psalm 36:5–6). The psalm ends by repeating verse 5. God is exalted.

1. How did the lofty praise of God bring resolution to the psalmist's struggle?
2. What are your favorite images in this psalm? How can you incorporate some of Psalm 57's language and style into your own prayer life?

FOUR

Psalm 59

Psalm 59 *Deliver me from my enemies, O God; be my fortress against those who are attacking me.* [2]*Deliver me from evildoers and save me from those who are after my blood.*

[3]*See how they lie in wait for me! Fierce men conspire against me for no offense or sin of mine, LORD.* [4]*I have done no wrong, yet they are ready to attack me. Arise to help me; look on my plight!* [5]*You, LORD God Almighty, you who are the God of Israel, rouse yourself to punish all the nations; show no mercy to wicked traitors.*

[6]*They return at evening, snarling like dogs, and prowl about the city.* [7]*See what they spew from their mouths—the words from their lips are sharp as swords, and they think, "Who can hear us?"* [8]*But you laugh at them, LORD; you scoff at all those nations.*

[9]You are my strength, I watch for you; you, God, are my fortress, [10]my God on whom I can rely.

God will go before me and will let me gloat over those who slander me. [11]But do not kill them, Lord our shield, or my people will forget. In your might uproot them and bring them down. [12]For the sins of their mouths, for the words of their lips, let them be caught in their pride. For the curses and lies they utter, [13]consume them in your wrath, consume them till they are no more. Then it will be known to the ends of the earth that God rules over Jacob.

[14]They return at evening, snarling like dogs, and prowl about the city. [15]They wander about for food and howl if not satisfied. [16]But I will sing of your strength, in the morning I will sing of your love; for you are my fortress, my refuge in times of trouble.

[17]You are my strength, I sing praise to you; you, God, are my fortress, my God on whom I can rely.

Key Observation. By releasing our true feelings in prayer, we can relinquish our desire for vengeance and remember God's mission.

Understanding the Word. Psalm 59 is a prayer for deliverance from enemies. Its heading references 1 Samuel 19:11–17, when Saul sent assassins to David's home in order to kill him the next morning. David escaped in the night with the help of his wife, Saul's daughter Michal. The language of Psalm 59 is intense. It models for us how to express deep emotions and desires for security from dangerous foes while still handing over to God our temptations to act violently in our strength. This is critical for growing spiritually by praying the Psalms. They do not shy away from violent language, but the psalmists *always* trust God to take action according to his character and will. The Psalms nowhere advocate personal violence or vengeance against one's enemies.

Psalm 59 unfolds in three sections: an opening petition and a description of trouble (vv. 1–5) followed by two sections of complaint and confession of trust (vv. 6–10, vv. 11–17).

In verses 1–5, the psalmist cried out to God for rescue. He needed protection. "Be my fortress" (v. 1) may also be translated "be exalted." The psalmist was crying out for God to be bigger and rise higher than those mortals bringing trouble. Verse 2 assumes that the psalmist's enemies are evil and bloodthirsty. The psalmist declared his innocence and the guilt of his adversaries in verses 3–5. God must act because of the injustice of the situation. This invites us always to reflect on our innocence when praying for God to act in our favor.

In the first section of complaint and trust (vv. 6–10), the psalmist compared his foes to wild dogs (vv. 6–7, cf. 14–15). In contrast, the psalmist trusted and praised God, who laughs at the nations who attempt to thwart God's mission (see Psalm 2:4). Rather than focusing on the dogs, the psalmist trusted the Lord in the full confidence that God would protect him and give him victory.

In verses 11–17 there is a more intense complaint. The psalmist asked that God pay his enemies fully for their evil actions. The language is personal and harsh. The psalmist had suffered much and desired to see his enemies suffer too. This is an honest and human expression given the circumstances. As Christians, we understand that we are to love our enemies and pray for them (see Matthew 5:44; Romans 12:14–21). This prayer helps us move toward this ideal by pushing us to relinquish our desire for vengeance to God. That is what the psalmist did. He wanted God's name to be known across the planet (v. 13).

Psalm 59 ends with the psalmist reaffirming a deep confidence and trust that God will protect him. The psalmist moved from complaint to praise. This was possible because of the psalmist's honesty in releasing his desires to God.

1. What do you think about the psalmist's violent request for God to take action against the psalmist's enemies?
2. How does this prayer help us learn to love and pray for our enemies?

FIVE

Psalm 60

Psalm 60 (ESV) *O God, you have rejected us, broken our defenses; you have been angry; oh, restore us.* [2]*You have made the land to quake; you have torn it open; repair its breaches, for it totters.* [3]*You have made your people see hard things; you have given us wine to drink that made us stagger.*

[4]*You have set up a banner for those who fear you, that they may flee to it from the bow. Selah* [5]*That your beloved ones may be delivered, give salvation by your right hand and answer us!*

[6]God has spoken in his holiness: "With exultation I will divide up Shechem and portion out the Vale of Succoth. [7]Gilead is mine; Manasseh is mine; Ephraim is my helmet; Judah is my scepter. [8]Moab is my washbasin; upon Edom I cast my shoe; over Philistia I shout in triumph."

[9]Who will bring me to the fortified city? Who will lead me to Edom? [10]Have you not rejected us, O God? You do not go forth, O God, with our armies. [11]Oh, grant us help against the foe, for vain is the salvation of man! [12]With God we shall do valiantly; it is he who will tread down our foes.

Key Observation. No matter the odds stacked against God's people, we can pray for God's justice and love during times of war.

Understanding the Word. Psalm 60 is a national lament for help against the nations of Edom, Moab, and Philistia. The heading links it to David's battles against enemies in Aram and Edom (see 2 Samuel 8:3–16; 10:6–13). When reading about Israel's wars, we must remember that Israel existed only by God's grace and power. Israel was a tiny nation in an insignificant part of the world. The major powers of Egypt and Mesopotamia surrounded it. Israel was always the underdog. It never enjoyed the overwhelming military and economic advantages that modern Western nations have today. Israel's only chance was for God to win the victory for them.

Psalm 60 opens with recognition of Israel's dependence on God (vv. 1–3). The psalmist feared that God had rejected his people because they had suffered defeat at the hands of their enemies. This loss is compared to the effects of an earthquake. It feels as though creation itself has come undone. The psalmist prayed for restoration. These words assume that God has ultimate control over the situation. This is a crucial word for us. We are not helpless as followers of Jesus before the crises facing our world. When we find ourselves as a community of faith surrounded on all sides, this prayer gives us language to cry out for help.

Verses 4–5 ask God to create a safe haven for his people and to grant victory over their enemies. The appeal to God's right hand is a way of talking about God as the warrior who fights for his people (see Exodus 15:5). The psalmist cried out for the God who defeated Egypt at the Red Sea to once again raise his right hand of salvation.

Verses 6–8 cite a promise of God from a past time of worship in the sanctuary. This is the promise upon which the psalmist based this prayer. In verses 6–7, God declared ownership over the lands in question in the prayer. God gave his people the land of Canaan, including lands east of the Jordan River. This was the inheritance of God's Old Testament people and the land out of which the good news about Jesus the Messiah would ultimately spread. For God's mission to bless the nations to succeed, God's people needed physical security. Thus God promised them protection. Verse 8 lists Israel's immediate neighbors to the east (Moab and Edom) and to the west (Philistia). In this promise, these foes were defeated.

Verses 9–12 bring this national prayer to a climax with some key lessons. First, God's people recognized their need for God's participation. There is no victory without God (vv. 9–10). Second, no human help was needed. God's people confessed their reliance only on God's activity. Like Psalm 59, Psalm 60 recognizes the need to relinquish military action to God.

1. How does this psalm teach God's people to pray during a time of war?
2. What warnings does it provide for us as citizens of God's kingdom who find ourselves living among the nations?

WEEK FOUR

GATHERING DISCUSSION OUTLINE

A. Open session in prayer.

B. View video for this week's reading.

C. What general impressions and thoughts do you have after considering the video and reading the daily writings on these Scriptures? What, specifically, did this week's psalms teach you about faith, life, and prayer?

D. Discuss selected questions from the daily readings. Always invite class members to share key insights or to raise questions that they found to be the most meaningful.

1. **KEY OBSERVATION (PSALM 55):** When we find ourselves in times of trial, we must release all of our concerns and feelings to the God whom we can trust.

   DISCUSSION QUESTION: Reflect on your ability to be 100-percent honest about your feelings and circumstances with God. Is this difficult or easy for you? Why or why not?

2. **KEY OBSERVATION (PSALM 56):** Trust rooted in gratitude releases us from fear and opens us to God's work.

   DISCUSSION QUESTION: Make a list of your deepest fears. How does this psalm help you overcome them?

3. **KEY OBSERVATION (PSALM 57):** Times of lament serve as opportunities to grow in our relationship with God through our praise of God's protection.

   DISCUSSION QUESTION: How did the lofty praise of God bring resolution to the psalmist's struggle?

4. **KEY OBSERVATION (PSALM 59):** By releasing our true feelings in prayer, we can relinquish our desire for vengeance and remember God's mission.

   DISCUSSION QUESTION: How does this prayer help us learn to love and pray for our enemies?

5. **KEY OBSERVATION (PSALM 60):** No matter the odds stacked against God's people, we can pray for God's justice and love during times of war.

   DISCUSSION QUESTION: How does this psalm teach God's people to pray during a time of war?

E. Close session with prayer.

WEEK FIVE

Book II: Psalms of David (Praise and Thanksgiving)

ONE

Psalm 63

Psalm 63 *You, God, are my God, earnestly I seek you; I thirst for you, my whole
being longs for you, in a dry and parched land where there is no water.*

*[2]I have seen you in the sanctuary and beheld your power and your glory.
[3]Because your love is better than life, my lips will glorify you. [4]I will praise you as
long as I live, and in your name I will lift up my hands. [5]I will be fully satisfied as
with the richest of foods; with singing lips my mouth will praise you.*

*[6]On my bed I remember you; I think of you through the watches of the night.
[7]Because you are my help, I sing in the shadow of your wings. [8]I cling to you; your
right hand upholds me.*

*[9]Those who want to kill me will be destroyed; they will go down to the depths
of the earth. [10]They will be given over to the sword and become food for jackals.*

*[11]But the king will rejoice in God; all who swear by God will glory in him,
while the mouths of liars will be silenced.*

Key Observation. Dynamic praise flows out of a recognition that God's presence is with us always.

Understanding the Word. This week our study shifts to a series of praise psalms to close out the Davidic section of Books II–III. The past two weeks we've reflected on laments that arose out of difficult seasons and times. The links to David reminded God's people that even Israel's greatest king experienced hardships in his life. But the depths of David's challenges did not diminish his faith. Instead, they inspired David's praise to reach greater heights. As we work through these psalms, recognize that their praise emerged out of difficult circumstances. They will invite us to reflect how our struggles and difficulties have impacted our growth in grace and faith in God.

Psalm 63 breaks into two sections: verses 1–5 and 6–11. The heading links with the time when David was hiding in the wilderness (see 1 Samuel 23:14–15; 24:1). Psalm 63 captures the power of remembering worship in the sanctuary and the dynamic reality of God's presence with us wherever we are. The psalmist wrote as Israel's king (v. 11).

Verse 1 opens in a way similar to Psalm 42:1. The psalmist declared his intention to seek God earnestly. He thirsted for God in the same way that a person in a desert longs for water. This longing for God emerged out of the depths of the psalmist's being. This deep longing for God had its roots in the psalmist's personal experiences of worship in the sanctuary (v. 2). The psalmist had tasted and felt the power and awesomeness of God.

In response to the psalmist's memories and longing, this prayer turns to praise (vv. 3–5). Beholding God leads to a desire to declare God's goodness. The psalmist's words were a testimony. He confidently vowed to praise God because he had found that an experience of God's steadfast and loyal love was better than life itself. Given this truth, the psalmist intended to speak words of blessing to God and raise up his hands in recognition of God's greatness as long as he lives. The psalmist's life will find its deepest satisfaction in showering praise upon the Lord.

In verses 6–11, the psalmist shifted from memories of profound worship in the sanctuary to an assurance and experience of God's presence and protection in the present. In verses 6–8, the psalmist remembered God and meditated through the night (cf. Psalm 1:2). Nighttime is often for worry and anxiety. Instead, the psalmist focused on God as his helper and imagined future times of worship in the sanctuary. The psalmist's life was secure because he clung to God.

Enemies threatened the psalmist (vv. 9–10), but God would defeat them. The psalmist would then lead the praise celebrating God's deliverance. This psalm reminds us that God is with us always. It also models a whole-being praise to God in all circumstances because God's salvation will prevail.

1. How would your life be different if you longed for God in the same way that the psalmist did?
2. How does Psalm 63 teach us to understand God's presence even when we may find ourselves in the wilderness?

TWO

Psalm 65

Psalm 65 (ESV) *Praise is due to you, O God, in Zion, and to you shall vows be performed. [2]O you who hear prayer, to you shall all flesh come. [3]When iniquities prevail against me, you atone for our transgressions. [4]Blessed is the one you choose and bring near, to dwell in your courts! We shall be satisfied with the goodness of your house, the holiness of your temple!*

[5]By awesome deeds you answer us with righteousness, O God of our salvation, the hope of all the ends of the earth and of the farthest seas; [6]the one who by his strength established the mountains, being girded with might; [7]who stills the roaring of the seas, the roaring of their waves, the tumult of the peoples, [8]so that those who dwell at the ends of the earth are in awe at your signs. You make the going out of the morning and the evening to shout for joy.

[9]You visit the earth and water it; you greatly enrich it; the river of God is full of water; you provide their grain, for so you have prepared it. [10]You water its furrows abundantly, settling its ridges, softening it with showers, and blessing its growth. [11]You crown the year with your bounty; your wagon tracks overflow with abundance. [12]The pastures of the wilderness overflow, the hills gird themselves with joy, [13]the meadows clothe themselves with flocks, the valleys deck themselves with grain, they shout and sing together for joy.

Key Observation. Gratitude flows from our recognition of the blessings and grace of God all around us.

Understanding the Word. Psalms 65–67 serve to remind us of the centrality of God's mission. The challenges of life can keep us focused narrowly on our needs. Our next three psalms invite us to look at the big picture. God's mission involves announcing to the nations the good news.

The gospel arrives in our lives on its way to someone else. Psalms 65–67 are a word to all people about the abundance God offers. Praise and thanksgiving remind God's people that God is the Lord of all creation. Its call for praise by all people points to the Psalter's concluding vision of a chorus of praise for the Lord (Psalms 146–150; cf. 150:6).

Psalm 65 is a celebration of God's faithfulness and reorients us with the blessings and goodness of life. This psalm overflows with gratitude for the gifts that God gives. It models for us how we pray to God with grateful hearts for all of God's gifts and blessings to us.

Verses 1–4 open with God's people acknowledging the debt of praise owed to God and their commitment to fulfill their vows. When we receive God's grace, we respond with praise and thanksgiving. Verse 2 affirms God's faithfulness in answering prayer. Our God is a God of relationships. God invites and hears our prayers as well as those of all people.

Before moving to focus on the blessings that God gives to the whole earth, the psalmist gave thanks to God for the gift of reconciliation and forgiveness. Verses 3–4 remind us that God says yes to us despite our sins and failings. God answers our prayers of confession and forgives us our sins because of his goodness and grace. Verse 4 recognizes that God's grace makes worship and enjoyment of God's presence possible. These opening verses show God's people gathered in God's presence to worship the Lord for the grace and abundance that he offers.

Verses 5–8 model how to show gratitude to God. The thanksgiving begins by focusing on God's power to save. God is a Deliverer and Savior. Verse 5 declares that God's salvation extends to the ends of the earth. This is good news for all people. Verses 6–8 offer reflections on God's power in creation to demonstrate that the God of the Bible is, indeed, Lord of all.

Verses 9–13 bring the thanksgiving to a close by describing the good world that God has made. God is not only a mighty Savior (vv. 5–8), but also a bountiful Provider. This final paragraph reminds us of the world's beauty and richness. In the Sermon on the Mount, Jesus will echo the implications of these words for understanding God's love for all: "He causes his sun to rise on the evil and the good, and sends rain on the righteous and the unrighteous" (Matt. 5:45).

1. Start practicing gratitude immediately. Write down five blessings that you have received from God this week.
2. Why is gratitude an important aspect of the life of faith? How does it help you personally?

THREE

Psalm 66

Psalm 66 *Shout for joy to God, all the earth! [2]Sing the glory of his name; make his praise glorious. [3]Say to God, "How awesome are your deeds! So great is your power that your enemies cringe before you. [4]All the earth bows down to you; they sing praise to you, they sing the praises of your name."*

[5]Come and see what God has done, his awesome deeds for mankind! [6]He turned the sea into dry land, they passed through the waters on foot—come, let us rejoice in him. [7]He rules forever by his power, his eyes watch the nations—let not the rebellious rise up against him.

[8]Praise our God, all peoples, let the sound of his praise be heard; [9]he has preserved our lives and kept our feet from slipping. [10]For you, God, tested us; you refined us like silver. [11]You brought us into prison and laid burdens on our backs. [12]You let people ride over our heads; we went through fire and water, but you brought us to a place of abundance.

[13]I will come to your temple with burnt offerings and fulfill my vows to you—[14]vows my lips promised and my mouth spoke when I was in trouble. [15]I will sacrifice fat animals to you and an offering of rams; I will offer bulls and goats.

[16]Come and hear, all you who fear God; let me tell you what he has done for me. [17]I cried out to him with my mouth; his praise was on my tongue. [18]If I had cherished sin in my heart, the Lord would not have listened; [19]but God has surely listened and has heard my prayer. [20]Praise be to God, who has not rejected my prayer or withheld his love from me!

Key Observation. The nations will praise God because of the testimonies of God's saving power by God's people.

Understanding the Word. When life is difficult, it is vital to lift our eyes and see the bright sky ahead. In Romans 13:11–12, Paul wrote these encouraging words to the church: "And do this, understanding the present time: The hour has already come for you to wake up from your slumber, because our salvation is nearer now than when we first believed. The night is nearly over; the day is almost here. So let us put aside the deeds of darkness and put on the armor of light." Psalm 66 reminds God's people of the good that is coming.

Psalm 66 envisions a day that we desire to see. It imagines the fulfillment of God's mission to bless the nations through the expansion of God's kingdom of love, peace, and justice across the planet. The psalmist issued a call to "all the earth" (vv. 1 and 4) to cheer loudly to God. Imagine the roar of the crowd at the introduction of a star player in a packed stadium. This is the sense of excitement with which the psalmist began.

The nations' worship was audacious. All peoples gathered to celebrate and worship loudly the victories of God.

Verses 5–7 ground the praise of God in the exodus from Egypt and crossing of the Red Sea (see Exodus 13:17–15:21). The New Testament equivalent is the life, death, and resurrection of Jesus. In other words, Psalm 66 teaches that God secured the future for his people in these foundational acts. God's people can live confidently and faithfully because he has already prevailed over the forces of evil.

The psalmist addressed the nations again in verses 8–12. The psalmist called on the peoples of the earth to bless God's name. This was to extend the honor and glory that God deserves as Savior. God's people then confessed how God had continued to sustain them even through times of trials and testing (vv. 9–12).

Sometimes it is tempting to label such claims as wishful thinking. This psalm will have none of that. In verses 13–20, the focus shifts from all the nations praising Israel's God for his past actions to an individual giving thanks to God for deliverance in the present. This move is vital. Faith is rooted in God's past actions and cultivates hope for God's good future, but faith sustains us in the present. This is the promise and testimony of Scripture.

In verses 13–15, the psalmist declared that he would fulfill his vows. This announced to the community that God has acted anew.

In verses 16–20, the psalmist shared his testimony of God's goodness and faithfulness. The psalmist prayed to God. God listened and acted on behalf of the psalmist. The psalmist publicly blessed God. There are a couple of critical lessons here. First, this psalm declares that God is worthy of praise because he continues to act for the good of his people. Second, the psalmist modeled the reality that every act of grace serves as an opportunity to witness to the world.

1. What is the basis for your hope for the future?
2. What does your testimony about God say to the world around you?

FOUR

Psalm 67

Psalm 67 (ESV) *May God be gracious to us and bless us and make his face to shine upon us, Selah [2]that your way may be known on earth, your saving power among all nations. [3]Let the peoples praise you, O God; let all the peoples praise you!*

[4]Let the nations be glad and sing for joy, for you judge the peoples with equity and guide the nations upon earth. Selah [5]Let the peoples praise you, O God; let all the peoples praise you!

[6]The earth has yielded its increase; God, our God, shall bless us. [7]God shall bless us; let all the ends of the earth fear him!

Key Observation. God blesses his people as a means of sharing these blessings with all people.

Understanding the Word. The book of Psalms is our prayer book as God's missional people. God's people serve as agents of blessing and as reflections of God's holy love in/to/for the world. Psalm 67 declares this truth. As we saw in Psalm 48, God is not for Israel *against* the nations, but rather, God is for Israel *for the sake of* the nations. Psalm 67 articulates a vision of the nations worshiping the Lord.

In the Old Testament world, the power of gods was demonstrated through the material prosperity of a nation. The prayer of this psalm is that the nations will come to know the Lord by seeing the good that he has brought to his people.

Verse 1 opens with words similar to the priestly blessing of Numbers 6:24–27. God's people use this priestly blessing as a prayer directly to God for his blessing. Verse 2 emphasizes that this request is mission driven rather than self-centered. It is no sign of spiritual depth to ask God for material blessings that only benefit us personally. The goal of this prayer is rich. God's people request his blessing so that God's way may be known. They desire to see knowledge of God's saving power among all nations.

Notice that there is a purpose for the spreading of knowledge. This knowledge will lead to action by the nations. They will praise God! All peoples will join God's people in praising God. This is the ultimate reason for mission.

This is an audacious vision for God's people. Too often we feel small and insignificant in comparison to the nations, parties, and other religions that surround us. Yet this prayer reminds us of our role in God's kingdom. From the calling of Abram until now, we are blessed to be a blessing (see Genesis 12:2–3).

Verses 4–5 call the nations to gladness, songs of joy, and praise to God. This call to a universal praise finds its basis in God's fairness and kindness to all people. God blesses his people so they can extend these blessings to others. There is no favoritism. God guides and judges the earth faithfully and predictably. This external focus on the nations is important for God's people. We've read many psalms that categorize outsiders as the enemy due to their actions against God's people. This psalm reminds us that the goal of the gospel is to shape a new world where all people celebrate and acknowledge the God who loves them.

Verses 6–7 conclude this prayer with an affirmation of God's ongoing blessings of his people. God is faithful and his faithfulness will continue.

Psalm 67 reminds us as followers of Jesus that the gospel comes into our lives on its way to other people in other places. God blesses us with love, peace, and joy so we can share those blessings with a world that desperately needs them.

1. How does Psalm 67 understand the mission of God's people in the world?
2. What are specific ways that you participate in extending the blessings of God to others in the world who do not yet follow Jesus?

FIVE

Psalm 72

Psalm 72 *Endow the king with your justice, O God, the royal son with your righteousness. [2]May he judge your people in righteousness, afflicted ones with justice.*

[3]May the mountains bring prosperity to the people, the hills the fruit of righteousness. [4]May he defend the afflicted among the people and save the children of the needy; may he crush the oppressor. [5]May he endure as long as the sun, as long as the moon, through all generations. [6]May he be like rain falling on a mown field, like showers watering the earth. [7]In his days may the righteous flourish and prosperity abound till the moon is no more.

[8]May he rule from sea to sea and from the River to the ends of the earth. [9]May the desert tribes bow before him and his enemies lick the dust. [10]May the kings of Tarshish and of distant shores bring tribute to him. May the kings of Sheba and Seba present him gifts. [11]May all kings bow down to him and all nations serve him.

[12]For he will deliver the needy who cry out, the afflicted who have no one to help. [13]He will take pity on the weak and the needy and save the needy from death. [14]He will rescue them from oppression and violence, for precious is their blood in his sight.

[15]Long may he live! May gold from Sheba be given him. May people ever pray for him and bless him all day long. [16]May grain abound throughout the land; on the tops of the hills may it sway. May the crops flourish like Lebanon and thrive like the grass of the field. [17]May his name endure forever; may it continue as long as the sun.

Then all nations will be blessed through him, and they will call him blessed.

[18]Praise be to the Lord *God, the God of Israel, who alone does marvelous deeds. [19]Praise be to his glorious name forever; may the whole earth be filled with his glory. Amen and Amen. [20]This concludes the prayers of David son of Jesse.*

Key Observation. God's kingdom extends his mercy, grace, justice, and love through the reign of the Messiah.

Understanding the Word. Psalm 72 is a key point of transition in the book of Psalms. It serves as the conclusion of Book II, and its final verse (v. 20) indicates the end of the psalms linked to David in Books I and II. Psalm 72 focuses on a prayer for the Davidic king (or messiah). God is the Creator and King of kings, but God chose the Davidic king to serve as God's visible agent to lead his kingdom on earth. This prayer reminds us, as followers of Jesus, of the kingdom that King Jesus has launched through his life, death, and resurrection. This prayer expresses our human longing for a different world—the world that God through the gospel is bringing into existence.

Verses 1–4 open this prayer with a vision and request for the ideal king. We all long for godly leadership that truly benefits all people. These verses describe such a leader. The psalmist requests one who embodies God's justice and righteousness. This is a vision that extends God's kindness and blessings to the least of these. This is a critical theme in Scripture. In Jesus' kingdom, justice is truly for all—especially for those oppressed, needy, and marginalized. Abundance is not merely for the rich and powerful. It extends to the poor. God stands against all forces of oppression that attempt to suffocate and choke the joy and life out of others.

How long will Jesus' reign last? Verses 5–11 envision a perpetual kingdom as stable as the sun and moon in the sky above. Abundance in the form of righteousness and peace will persist (vv. 7–8). Jesus' reign will expand to the ends of the earth. Threats and enemies will vanish before him (vv. 9–11). Former foes will become worshipers and offerers of tribute.

Verses 12–14 remind us again of the kind of kingdom that God desires. It is one that extends kindness to all. The gospel is for those desperate for what only God can truly provide. As God's people, we have the opportunity to embody this vision by acting mercifully toward the poor and excluded.

Verses 15–17 conclude the prayer for the king with final pleas for his longevity and success. Note again the missional theme from this week's psalms in verse 17b—the psalmist prays for the blessing of the nations.

Of course, all of this is possible because the Lord, the God of Israel, makes it so. Verses 18–19 invite God's people to bless and worship the Lord, who does great things.

As we pray these words, let us be mindful of the opening lines of Jesus' model prayer: "Our father in heaven, hallowed be your name, your kingdom come, your will be done, on earth as it is in heaven" (Matt. 6:9–10) as well as the closing prayer of Revelation: "Come, Lord Jesus!" (Rev. 22:20b).

1. What does Psalm 72 teach us about the nature and character of God's kingdom?
2. How does Psalm 72 teach us to pray about the future?

WEEK FIVE

GATHERING DISCUSSION OUTLINE

A. Open session in prayer.

B. View video for this week's reading.

C. What general impressions and thoughts do you have after considering the video and reading the daily writings on these Scriptures? What, specifically, did this week's psalms teach you about faith, life, and prayer?

D. Discuss selected questions from the daily readings. Always invite class members to share key insights or to raise questions that they found to be the most meaningful.

1. **KEY OBSERVATION (PSALM 63):** Dynamic praise flows out of a recognition that God's presence is with us always.

   DISCUSSION QUESTION: How does Psalm 63 teach us to understand God's presence even when we may find ourselves in the wilderness?

2. **KEY OBSERVATION (PSALM 65):** Gratitude flows from our recognition of the blessings and grace of God all around us.

   DISCUSSION QUESTION: Why is gratitude an important aspect of the life of faith? How does it help you personally?

3. **KEY OBSERVATION (PSALM 66):** The nations will praise God because of the testimonies of God's saving power by God's people.

   DISCUSSION QUESTION: What does your testimony about God say to the world around you?

4. **KEY OBSERVATION (PSALM 67):** God blesses his people as a means of sharing these blessings with all people.

   DISCUSSION QUESTION: What are specific ways that you participate in extending the blessings of God to others in the world who do not yet follow Jesus?

5. **KEY OBSERVATION (PSALM 72):** God's kingdom extends his mercy, grace, justice, and love through the reign of the Messiah.

   DISCUSSION QUESTION: What does Psalm 72 teach us about the nature and character of God's kingdom?

E. Close session with prayer.

WEEK SIX

Book III: Trials and Transformation in the Psalms of Asaph

ONE

Psalm 73:1–12

Psalm 73:1–12 (ESV) *Truly God is good to Israel, to those who are pure in heart. [2]But as for me, my feet had almost stumbled, my steps had nearly slipped. [3]For I was envious of the arrogant when I saw the prosperity of the wicked.*

[4]For they have no pangs until death; their bodies are fat and sleek. [5]They are not in trouble as others are; they are not stricken like the rest of mankind. [6]Therefore pride is their necklace; violence covers them as a garment. [7]Their eyes swell out through fatness; their hearts overflow with follies. [8]They scoff and speak with malice; loftily they threaten oppression. [9]They set their mouths against the heavens, and their tongue struts through the earth. [10]Therefore his people turn back to them, and find no fault in them. [11]And they say, "How can God know? Is there knowledge in the Most High?" [12]Behold, these are the wicked; always at ease, they increase in riches.

Key Observation. People of faith may experience crises when their understanding of God's goodness does not match their experiences of life.

Understanding the Word. This week we will explore Psalms 73 and 77. These psalms are critical for building a sure foundation for life and faith in the midst of trouble. Although these psalms offer no easy answers, they do point the way forward when life stops making sense. Personally, these psalms have greatly impacted my life and sustained me at key moments.

Psalm 73 marks a critical point in the book of Psalms. Psalm 73 narrates a crisis of faith and its renewal. It stands at the beginning of Book III, approximately in the middle of the Psalter. It tells a story that includes a lament, a response by God, and a grateful psalmist fully practicing a dynamic faith. Scholars debate the precise nature of Psalm 73, but it presents the life experience of the psalmist and offers wisdom and instruction for the community of faith.

Psalm 73 unfolds in three movements: crisis (vv. 1–12), turning point (vv. 13–17), and resolution (vv. 18–28). The psalm opens with a proverb that sounds like a statement of faith: "Truly God is good to Israel, to those who are pure in heart." In the New Testament, Paul wrote, "And we know that for those who love God all things work together for good, for those who are called according to his purpose" (Rom. 8:28 ESV). In our day, we often affirm, "God is good all the time; all the time God is good." In the big-picture view of Scripture and life, all of these statements are *true*. The problem occurs in seasons of life when God's goodness is not obvious or felt. This is the issue at the heart of the psalm.

Verses 2–3 describe the problem the psalmist faced. It is a crisis of faith. In contrast to the optimism of verse 1, the psalmist declared how his feet almost slipped. In other words, he came close to losing his faith. The reason was simple. His view of God's goodness diminished because he became jealous and envious of the seeming prosperity of the wicked. How can the wicked, who live far from God, appear happier and more prosperous than a faithful member of God's people?

Verses 4–12 go into specific detail about the psalmist's observations of the well-being of the wicked. The psalmist's plight is a common one. We gravitate to faith in part for *security*. But what happens when our faith does not translate to a material life better than that of those who pay no attention to the things of God?

The psalmist observed that the wicked have no struggles but instead enjoy plenty of food and increasing power. Yet they practice evil. They are prideful, gluttonous, full of evil intentions, and irreverent toward God. These realities made no sense to the psalmist. He struggled, lacked resources, and felt powerless *despite* his commitments to living faithfully to the God of Israel, whom he confessed is good to the faithful.

1. Reflect on times in your life when you struggled in your faith due to hardships and suffering.
2. What parts of the Bible or gospel are the most difficult to believe when you are going through challenging times?

TWO

Psalm 73:13–17

Psalm 73:13–17 (ESV) *All in vain have I kept my heart clean and washed my hands in innocence. [14]For all the day long I have been stricken and rebuked every morning. [15]If I had said, "I will speak thus," I would have betrayed the generation of your children.*

[16]But when I thought how to understand this, it seemed to me a wearisome task, [17]until I went into the sanctuary of God; then I discerned their end.

Key Observation. Our Christian community is critical for sustaining us during dark nights of the soul.

Understanding the Word. In verses 13–17, the psalmist's plight reached its climax and took a turn toward resolution. Verses 13–16 present a conflicted psalmist. He was confused, frustrated, and close to falling away. Yet he remembered the faithful members of his community.

Verse 13 opens with "all in vain." This phrase actually contains the same word translated "truly" in verse 1 (ESV; cf. v. 18). Its repetition breaks the psalm into three sections, but it also serves to emphasize the opening statement of each of the sections. If verse 1 was a confession of God's goodness, then verse 13 confesses the psalmist's assessment of his faith during this crisis. The psalmist gave us a transcript of his thoughts. He concluded that faith in God had been in vain. Attempts to live faithfully did not lead to abundance in comparison with the prosperity of the wicked.

Verse 14 describes the cause of the psalmist's anguish. There is a disconnect between received faith ("Truly God is good to Israel . . . ," v. 1) and the lack of evidence of it in the psalmist's life. He teeters on the border between belief and unbelief.

But the psalmist resisted the urge to publicly confess his doubts (v. 15). What caused his hesitation? It was not his faith in God. His faith was wavering. Rather, it was the community around him that held him. Verses 3–12 listed all of the observations that the psalmist made regarding the prosperity of the wicked. Verse 15 does not tell us anything specific about the community of faith, but it is clear that it was tight-knit and faithful. The psalmist remembered the "generation of your children" and refused to betray their way of life. This points to the crucial role of the Christ-following community in encouraging and caring for one another. There will be dark times of our souls when only fellow believers will keep us rooted. This is part of the faith journey. Our community makes God's reality visible, especially in times when God's activity is invisible to us.

The tension between his thoughts about the wicked and his commitment to his community reached its climax in verse 16. The psalmist was unable to resolve the dilemma by relying on his intelligence or reason. Psalm 73 suggests a different path. In verse 17, the psalmist informs us that renewal came during a visit to the sanctuary. He does not tell us the details. The key was that despite his crisis of faith, he went to the temple and experienced a life-changing moment of clarity. Was it the music? Was it the singing? Was it watching others worship? Was it the words and acts of the priests and Levites? Was it the smell of the burnt offering? The psalmist doesn't tell us. The verse invites us to use our imaginations, put ourselves into the psalmist's situation, and reflect on how we meet God in our places of worship.

1. Who in your life models faithfulness and strength to you?
2. What do you think happened to the psalmist when he entered the temple?
3. What parts of worship speak the most meaningfully to you?

THREE

Psalm 73:18–28

Psalm 73:18–28 (ESV) *Truly you set them in slippery places; you make them fall to ruin.* [19]*How they are destroyed in a moment, swept away utterly by terrors!*

[20]Like a dream when one awakes, O Lord, when you rouse yourself, you despise
them as phantoms. [21]When my soul was embittered, when I was pricked in heart,
[22]I was brutish and ignorant; I was like a beast toward you.

[23]Nevertheless, I am continually with you; you hold my right hand. [24]You
guide me with your counsel, and afterward you will receive me to glory. [25]Whom
have I in heaven but you? And there is nothing on earth that I desire besides you.
[26]My flesh and my heart may fail, but God is the strength of my heart and my
portion forever.

[27]For behold, those who are far from you shall perish; you put an end to
everyone who is unfaithful to you. [28]But for me it is good to be near God; I have
made the Lord GOD my refuge, that I may tell of all your works.

Key Observation. When we see the world as God does, we experience transformation and become ambassadors of this good news.

Understanding the Word. Psalm 73:18–28 narrates the psalmist's reorientation following his transformative encounter in the sanctuary. Recall the psalmist's story thus far. It begins with a truth affirmed by his community: "Truly God is good" (v. 1 ESV) and his confession of his near fall from grace (v. 2). This moves to a description of his problem (vv. 3–12). He envied the wicked, who lived far from God. He asked, in so many words, "How can they prosper in their unbelief while I struggle despite my faith?" Verses 13–17 serve as a catalyst for renewal. The psalmist could not answer his question, but he refused to give up or to announce his fears publicly out of respect for his faithful friends. Instead, he entered the sanctuary. In a transforming moment, he went from doubt, despair, complaint, and scarcity to renewed faith, hope, praise, and abundance.

Verses 18–28 give us details of his transformation. In verses 18–20, the truth about the wicked emerges. Present blessing is no indicator of one's eternal security and destiny. For the faithful, it is crucial to remember God. God does not change the world through coercion and blasts of wrath. In Jesus, God sowed seeds of the victory of love, peace, joy, and abundance. The kingdom advanced through Jesus' service to the broken, his sacrificial death on the cross, and God's resurrection of Jesus from the grave. In the moment, Jesus was dead and the wicked were prosperous and triumphant, but God had other ideas. As Christians, we can maintain faith in the face of setbacks because God has acted to guarantee the future.

The psalmist had a similar experience. In the sanctuary, the psalmist gained a new perspective. In the end, God's love will prevail. The only guarantee for the future is to embrace the life of faith and turn away from the practices of the wicked.

Recognizing this truth, the psalmist confessed his prior bitterness and foolishness to God (vv. 21–22). There is good news for us here. God did not reject the psalmist. The psalmist was able to bring his brokenness and share his teetering faith with God. This led to the psalmist's renewal of faith and recognition of God's presence despite the psalmist's experienced lack of prosperity when compared to the wicked (vv. 23–26). The psalmist then realized God's presence was there all along. This can be our experience as well.

Crises of faith will come. Psalm 73 reminds us that they can serve as catalysts for growth in grace. The psalmist discovered God's real presence in his life and recognized the strength and security in the Lord. He did not need to fear or envy the wicked. They stood on shaky ground.

The psalm ends powerfully with verse 28. In it the psalmist made two key declarations: (1) God is indeed good. The community affirmation of verse 1 was now the psalmist's heartfelt personal confession. (2) The psalmist embraced the mission of God as the focus of life. He would announce publicly the good news about God. By embracing mission, the psalmist was completely renewed.

1. How did the psalmist's perspective change through the course of the psalm?
2. What was the connection between the psalmist's renewal and God's mission?

FOUR

Psalm 77:1–12

Psalm 77:1–12 *I cried out to God for help; I cried out to God to hear me.* [2]*When I was in distress, I sought the Lord; at night I stretched out untiring hands, and I would not be comforted.*

[3]I remembered you, God, and I groaned; I meditated, and my spirit grew faint. [4]You kept my eyes from closing; I was too troubled to speak. [5]I thought about the former days, the years of long ago; [6]I remembered my songs in the night. My heart meditated and my spirit asked:

[7]"Will the Lord reject forever? Will he never show his favor again? [8]Has his unfailing love vanished forever? Has his promise failed for all time? [9]Has God forgotten to be merciful? Has he in anger withheld his compassion?"

[10]Then I thought, "To this I will appeal: the years when the Most High stretched out his right hand. [11]I will remember the deeds of the Lord; yes, I will remember your miracles of long ago. [12]I will consider all your works and meditate on all your mighty deeds."

Key Observation. The way through a crisis of faith is to return to the foundations of our faith.

Understanding the Word. Psalm 77 is a bold cry for help. It narrates a crisis of faith similar to that found in Psalm 73. The psalmist dealt with a personal struggle or perhaps was suffering during a national calamity.

Verses 1–3 sounds similar to many of the laments we read. The psalmist recognized that God was the only source of hope, but God was not answering. Sometimes our faith can cause us pain beyond the suffering that we are already experiencing. The psalmist never explained the specifics of his situation, but it had morphed into a faith crisis. The psalmist did all the right things: he turned to God; he prayed without ceasing; he thought and meditated on God. But he received no resolution. The psalmist struggled with the pain of his situation and the pain of God's absence. Have you ever been in a similar place?

In verses 4–9, the psalmist pondered the meaning of God's silence. He did not understand God's absence. In fact, the psalmist wondered openly if God had somehow shifted from his previous ways of faithful love, committed promise, compassion, and mercy. He was comparing his understanding of God's dramatic actions in the past with his silence in the present. As we will see in the second half of the psalm, the psalmist remembered the exodus from Egypt. In the exodus, the Lord delivered God's people powerfully and decisively out of slavery, led them through the wilderness, and gifted them the land of Canaan. In the questions raised in verses 7–9, the psalmist mentioned key words that described the inner character of the Lord ("unfailing love," "merciful," "compassion," "favor"). God used similar wording of himself when he spoke to Moses at Sinai. In Exodus 34:6–7a, the Lord said, "The LORD, the LORD, the compassionate and gracious God, slow to anger, abounding in love and faithfulness, maintaining love to thousands, and forgiving wickedness, rebellion and sin." This declaration burned in the psalmist's mind. The faith of Israel depended on God acting consistently according to his revealed character. In Psalm 77, a deep fear began to dawn inside of the psalmist—the fear that the God of his ancestors had somehow changed due to God's anger at his people.

This fear would be equivalent to a Christian suddenly wondering if the Holy Spirit had departed or if Jesus' death had lost its saving power. The psalmist was in deep crisis. How would he move forward?

In verses 10–12, the psalmist made the bold decision to dig deeper in his faith. These verses focus on the psalmist's resolution to remember and focus on God's mighty acts in the past. The implication for the psalmist was that God would again act decisively and lovingly on his behalf and on behalf of all God's people. Despite the psalmist's doubts, he doubled down on his faith.

1. Reflect on a time in your life when God seemed absent. How did you respond?
2. What are your expectations of God during crisis? What is the basis for your expectations?

FIVE

Psalm 77:13-20

Psalm 77:13–20 *Your ways, God, are holy. What god is as great as our God?* [14]*You are the God who performs miracles; you display your power among the peoples.* [15]*With your mighty arm you redeemed your people, the descendants of Jacob and Joseph.*

[16]*The waters saw you, God, the waters saw you and writhed; the very depths were convulsed.* [17]*The clouds poured down water, the heavens resounded with thunder; your arrows flashed back and forth.* [18]*Your thunder was heard in the whirlwind, your lightning lit up the world; the earth trembled and quaked.* [19]*Your*

path led through the sea, your way through the mighty waters, though your footprints were not seen.

[20]*You led your people like a flock by the hand of Moses and Aaron.*

Key observation. Sacred memory, worship, community, and Scripture are core resources for renewal.

Understanding the Word. Psalm 77 shifts dramatically at verse 13. The psalmist's circumstances did not change. But the psalmist experienced an inner shift of perspective that transformed him from anxiety to confidence for the journey.

What changed for the psalmist? In verses 13–20, the psalmist moved from self-focus to a renewed focus on God, the future, and his community of faith. In verses 11–12, the psalmist declared his intention to meditate on God's past actions. Verses 13–20 offer us the content of his thoughts. His words model a pathway through trials for us too.

First, all of the "I" language from verses 1–12 disappears. In verses 1–12, the psalmist focused on himself. At verse 13, the psalmist addressed God directly. He engaged God in conversation rather than replaying endless cycles of worst-case scenarios in his mind. To move out of crisis, we need to shift from "I" language to "you" language, especially when the "you" is the God who saves.

Second, the psalmist focused on God's awesome past deeds. In verses 16–20, the psalmist remembered God's powerful deliverance of his people in the exodus. The implication for the psalmist was clear. The Lord could be trusted in the present crisis, and God has complete control over the future. As Christians, we can stand on the life, death, and resurrection of Jesus in addition to the mighty actions that God showed in the Old Testament.

Third, the psalmist moved from treating God merely as an object. He was having a theological crisis in verses 1–12. His understanding of God did not make sense because of his present experience. In verses 13–20, the psalmist moved from theological reflection to an experience of God's presence through remembering and celebrating what God had already done.

Fourth, the psalmist recognized that he was part of something bigger than himself. He was a member of a worshiping community. He was not alone. In verses 13–20, there is a recurring focus on all God's people (vv. 14, 15, and 20).

Just as in Psalm 73, the experience and memory of our community served a key role in the psalmist's transformation.

Fifth, the psalmist shifted from lament to worship. Verses 13–20 end the psalm with a celebration of God's past actions. Moreover, it is in the remembrance of the past that the psalmist found his way forward. Verse 20 mentions Moses and Aaron. For Israel, this was a reminder of two key resources that these leaders represented: Scripture and the temple. The psalmist still had access to Moses' wisdom through the Scripture and to Aaron's leadership through participation in worship.

We have these privileges at our disposal today. Tough times will come. Psalms 73 and 77 serve as models for growing in grace during such times.

1. How, specifically, do verses 13–20 model a way through crisis for us?
2. What are your key learnings about faith in difficult circumstances from reading Psalms 73 and 77?

WEEK SIX

GATHERING DISCUSSION OUTLINE

A. Open session in prayer.

B. View video for this week's reading.

C. What general impressions and thoughts do you have after considering the video and reading the daily writings on these Scriptures? What, specifically, did this week's psalms teach you about faith, life, and prayer?

D. Discuss selected questions from the daily readings. Always invite class members to share key insights or to raise questions that they found to be the most meaningful.

1. **KEY OBSERVATION (PSALM 73:1–12):** People of faith may experience crises when their understanding of God's goodness does not match their experiences of life.

   DISCUSSION QUESTION: What parts of the Bible or gospel are the most difficult to believe when you are going through challenging times?

2. **KEY OBSERVATION (PSALM 73:13–17):** Our Christian community is critical for sustaining us during dark nights of the soul.

   DISCUSSION QUESTION: Who in your life models faithfulness and strength to you?

3. **KEY OBSERVATION (PSALM 73:18–28):** When we see the world as God does, we experience transformation and become ambassadors of this good news.

DISCUSSION QUESTION: What was the connection between the psalmist's renewal and God's mission?

4. **KEY OBSERVATION (PSALM 77:1–12):** The way through a crisis of faith is to return to the foundations of our faith.

   DISCUSSION QUESTION: Reflect on a time in your life when God seemed absent. How did you respond?

5. **KEY OBSERVATION (PSALM 77:13–20):** Sacred memory, worship, community, and Scripture are core resources for renewal.

   DISCUSSION QUESTION: How, specifically, do verses 13–20 model a way through crisis for us?

E. Close session with prayer.

WEEK SEVEN

Book III: Resources for Facing Catastrophe in the Songs of Asaph and Korah

ONE

Psalm 82

Psalm 82 (ESV) *God has taken his place in the divine council; in the midst of the gods he holds judgment:* [2]*"How long will you judge unjustly and show partiality to the wicked? Selah* [3]*Give justice to the weak and the fatherless; maintain the right of the afflicted and the destitute.* [4]*Rescue the weak and the needy; deliver them from the hand of the wicked."*

[5]*They have neither knowledge nor understanding, they walk about in darkness; all the foundations of the earth are shaken.*

[6]*I said, "You are gods, sons of the Most High, all of you;* [7]*nevertheless, like men you shall die, and fall like any prince."*

[8]*Arise, O God, judge the earth; for you shall inherit all the nations!*

Key Observation. The true mark of faithfulness is the practice of justice and mercy toward the marginalized.

Understanding the Word. This week's lessons combine two psalms of Asaph (82–83) and three psalms of Korah (84, 85, and 87). These psalms reflect on the crises God's people face. The world does not always work out the way we desire. God calls us to live holy lives as agents of blessing to the world. This life of mission does not immunize us against suffering. In fact, as we navigate Book III, the challenges portrayed in these psalms only increase.

Psalm 82 is a countercultural proclamation of justice and judgment. It is a prayer that the values of God's kingdom will manifest in our world. We long for love, hope, kindness, compassion, fairness, and equality for all people. Yet the news continually reminds us of the suffering and injustice experienced by many. How are we as God's people to serve as agents of God's abundance in such a world?

Verse 1 opens with a scene from a heavenly court. God, our Creator and Savior, presides over the gods and goddesses of the world. This psalm is not suggesting that there really are other gods. The Lord is the one true God, and the Bible as a whole proclaims this truth. The problem is that humanity creates many gods to compete with the Lord. What do we worship today? Security, affluence, military power, political ideologies, education, sex, family, possessions, status . . . just to name a few. This list contains both positive and negative elements. The danger occurs when we elevate any of these above our commitment to the true God. When this occurs, problems arise.

God asks all of the other gods a key question in verse 2. He puts justice and fairness forward as the key criteria for judgment. The Bible insists that when we elevate anyone or anything above God, injustice and wickedness will follow. Unfortunately, this has been the consistent pattern of human history.

God offers exhortations to the gods in verses 3–5. What matters is how we treat those on the margins (the poor, the sick, the weak, the lowly, the orphan, the widow, and the immigrant). Verses 3–4 exhort the "gods" to practice justice and to rescue the marginalized. This is the mark of true religion. Verse 5 diagnoses the true problem with our world. Those in power, as well as those elevated as gods, are lost themselves. Their injustice and inability to act rightly for all causes the fabric of society and the world itself to shake.

God, therefore, passes judgment on those gods who practice injustice (vv. 6–7). Their rule and lives will come to an end. There will be a day of reckoning for those who have used power unjustly for evil.

Psalm 82 ends with a prayer that calls for God to act as the true and legitimate King of creation. Verse 8 is an Old Testament way of God's people praying, "Your kingdom come, O Lord." May it come quickly.

1. How does this psalm teach us to pray for justice?

2. What are the marks of a just world? As God's people, how can we participate in its making?

TWO

Psalm 83

Psalm 83 (ESV) *O God, do not keep silence; do not hold your peace or be still, O God! [2]For behold, your enemies make an uproar; those who hate you have raised their heads. [3]They lay crafty plans against your people; they consult together against your treasured ones. [4]They say, "Come, let us wipe them out as a nation; let the name of Israel be remembered no more!" [5]For they conspire with one accord; against you they make a covenant—[6]the tents of Edom and the Ishmaelites, Moab and the Hagrites, [7]Gebal and Ammon and Amalek, Philistia with the inhabitants of Tyre; [8]Asshur also has joined them; they are the strong arm of the children of Lot. Selah*

[9]Do to them as you did to Midian, as to Sisera and Jabin at the river Kishon, [10]who were destroyed at En-dor, who became dung for the ground. [11]Make their nobles like Oreb and Zeeb, all their princes like Zebah and Zalmunna, [12]who said, "Let us take possession for ourselves of the pastures of God."

[13]O my God, make them like whirling dust, like chaff before the wind. [14]As fire consumes the forest, as the flame sets the mountains ablaze, [15]so may you pursue them with your tempest and terrify them with your hurricane!

[16]Fill their faces with shame, that they may seek your name, O LORD. [17]Let them be put to shame and dismayed forever; let them perish in disgrace, [18]that they may know that you alone, whose name is the LORD, are the Most High over all the earth.

Key Observation. When threatened by enemies, God's people pray for protection, but also for the salvation of those opposing them.

Understanding the Word. Psalm 83 is a lament by God's people for deliverance from the nations surrounding Israel. This is a national prayer. It envisions all of God's people praying to the Lord in the face of an impending invasion and national disaster. The future of God's mission to bless all peoples is at stake.

Verses 1–2 open the psalm with a cry to God to take action. God's people were in a desperate situation in which their enemies threatened them. The psalm assumes that enemies of God's people are enemies of God. As we pray this prayer, we must examine ourselves carefully. The psalmist assumed the innocence of God's people. But he also assumed the helplessness of God's people apart from God's actions. This is not a prayer of a powerful and militarily prepared people against weaker nations. This was a defenseless nation praying for deliverance from enemies hell-bent on their destruction.

Verses 3–8 specify the threat against God's people. Nations had plotted to wipe out God's people so that the name Israel would no longer be remembered (vv. 3–4). In other words, God's mission was at stake. Israel, as God's people, was the agent of blessing to the world, even to the enemies striking against it. Verses 5–8 list ten nations—including the superpower Asshur, or Assyria—plotting the destruction of God's people. The mention of Assyria makes it possible to date the psalm to between 740 and 612 BC, when Assyria was the dominant power. The names, however, are not as significant as the number ten. In Scripture, ten often represents completeness. This prayer is not only about the Assyrians and nine other countries allied against God's people. By listing ten threats, the psalmist was symbolizing the entire world lined up to threaten God's people and his mission to bless all peoples to the ends of the earth.

How do God's people pray when threatened on all sides? It is vital to hear the last half of the psalm (vv. 9–18) as more than a call to destroy Israel's enemies. It is a plea to save God's people for the sake of the salvation of the world. In verses 9–12, the psalmist asked God to act as he did for Israel during the time of the Judges. The specific references are to victories recorded in Judges 4–5; 7:25; and 8:1–21.

In the final section (vv. 13–18), the psalmist called for God to rise up as a powerful storm and demonstrate his power over the enemies. Yet in verses 16–18 we find a deeper prayer than one for destruction and vengeance. The psalmist desired a turning to the Lord by the enemies of God's people. In verses 16–17, the psalmist wanted to see Israel's enemies put to shame so that they lay down their pride and seek the Lord. Verse 18 brings this request to a climax by calling for a future acknowledgment of the Lord's reign from on high over all of the earth.

1. How does Psalm 83 teach God's people to pray when threatened by enemies?
2. How does the importance of God's mission shine through even in times of danger?

THREE

Psalm 84

Psalm 84 (ESV) *How lovely is your dwelling place, O LORD of hosts!* [2]*My soul longs, yes, faints for the courts of the LORD; my heart and flesh sing for joy to the living God.*

[3]*Even the sparrow finds a home, and the swallow a nest for herself, where she may lay her young, at your altars, O LORD of hosts, my King and my God.* [4]*Blessed are those who dwell in your house, ever singing your praise! Selah*

[5]*Blessed are those whose strength is in you, in whose heart are the highways to Zion.* [6]*As they go through the Valley of Baca they make it a place of springs; the early rain also covers it with pools.* [7]*They go from strength to strength; each one appears before God in Zion.*

[8]*O LORD God of hosts, hear my prayer; give ear, O God of Jacob! Selah* [9]*Behold our shield, O God; look on the face of your anointed!*

[10]*For a day in your courts is better than a thousand elsewhere. I would rather be a doorkeeper in the house of my God than dwell in the tents of wickedness.* [11]*For the LORD God is a sun and shield; the LORD bestows favor and honor. No good thing does he withhold from those who walk uprightly.* [12]*O LORD of hosts, blessed is the one who trusts in you!*

Key Observation. The memory and practice of God's presence fuels a meaningful and happy life.

Understanding the Word. Psalm 84 reorients us to the power of God's presence for sustaining us. Psalm 84 has inspired contemporary music and stirs hearts with its story of a pilgrimage to the temple. It is a psalm of Korah and is similar to the initial Korah psalms (Pss. 42–43). This psalm reminds us that worship is central to the life of faith.

Psalm 84 opens with the psalmist reflecting on the temple (vv. 1–4). The psalmist longed for God's presence. The visible beauty of the temple filled the psalmist with astonishment as he approached Jerusalem. He gazed upon the temple and anticipated its abundance. However, the temple's appearance was secondary to the reality that stood behind it. The psalmist desired to meet God. Verse 2 uses "my soul," "my heart," and "[my] flesh" to indicate the whole-being response of the psalmist. The psalmist worshiped the "living God." God is no inanimate object or distant presence. The God of Scripture is alive and near to us. Verse 3 reflects on God's open arms to all creation (cf. Psalm 36:6–7). Even birds can nest safely within God's house. Yet this welcoming God is the true King and God of the world. Our God is powerful, yet desires relationships with all creation. This is good news. The psalmist captured this with the first of a series of blessings (v. 4; cf. vv. 5 and 12). Those who dwell in the temple are the happy ones!

Verses 5–7 capture the joy of the psalmist's journey to Jerusalem. Who are the happy ones? Those who are moving toward God's temple, whether literally or in their hearts. These verses capture the joy and strength of worshipers as they march to the temple. If you've ever had a powerful experience of God in a particular place, you have a sense of the psalmist's feelings of renewal and strength.

In verses 8–9 the psalmist paused his own reflection and prayed for God's people. The psalmist, who longed for God, then began a conversation with God. He moved from focusing on his experiences to asking for God's blessings on the king, the "anointed." This reminds us that in personal experiences of God we must not neglect prayers for others. By praying for God's anointed, the psalmist asked for God's blessing on all God's people. as the king represents the whole.

The psalm concludes memorably in verses 10–12. The psalmist exclaimed the superiority of a life lived in the presence of God over any other. Verse 10 has inspired many to find purpose in all seasons and types of work. When we commune with God, life has meaning. Verse 11 reminds us of God's heart. God desires our best; he always has our best interests at heart.

How do we respond to the beauty of God's temple and richness of his blessings? Verse 12 exhorts us to find ourselves among the happy ones who fully trust God.

1. This psalm invites us to reflect on our journeys of faith. What places do you associate with deep experiences of God's grace?
2. How does the psalmist's enthusiasm about God's presence help you understand the happy life?

FOUR

Psalm 85

Psalm 85 *You, Lord, showed favor to your land; you restored the fortunes of Jacob. [2]You forgave the iniquity of your people and covered all their sins. [3]You set aside all your wrath and turned from your fierce anger.*

[4]Restore us again, God our Savior, and put away your displeasure toward us. [5]Will you be angry with us forever? Will you prolong your anger through all generations? [6]Will you not revive us again, that your people may rejoice in you? [7]Show us your unfailing love, Lord, and grant us your salvation.

[8]I will listen to what God the Lord says; he promises peace to his people, his faithful servants—but let them not turn to folly. [9]Surely his salvation is near those who fear him, that his glory may dwell in our land.

[10]Love and faithfulness meet together; righteousness and peace kiss each other. [11]Faithfulness springs forth from the earth, and righteousness looks down from heaven. [12]The Lord will indeed give what is good, and our land will yield its harvest. [13]Righteousness goes before him and prepares the way for his steps.

Key Observation. When in need of restoration, turn with reverence and prayer to the God of love, mercy, faithfulness, and compassion.

Understanding the Word. While Psalm 84 reoriented us with God's presence, Psalm 85 returns us to a chaotic world in need of God's salvation. Psalm 85 is a prayer for restoration and revival. These words teach us how to pray in a crisis when God seems silent.

Verses 1–3 open the psalm with recollections of the Lord's goodness. God's people have experienced dark times before. The Lord responded with restoration and forgiveness. God's people had felt God's anger for sin and unfaithfulness, but in the past, God always acted to bring revival and a renewed prosperity. These memories provided the confidence for the community to pray out of their present desperate need for renewal.

Verses 4–7 call on God to take action. The community assumes that God's character is loving, merciful, and gracious (cf. Exodus 34:6–7a). This is not a prayer by people in rebellion against God's ways. God's people have returned wholeheartedly to God. They are committed to the relationship. They wait for God, but they pray that he will act soon. What is it that God's people desire? They want renewal and the experience of God's loyal love in the present. They desire restoration to wholeness as individuals and as a community so that they may again rejoice in God. The assumption is that the highest joy in life is a vital moment-by-moment relationship with the Lord. The community wants nothing more than what they declared in their prayers.

In verses 8–9, the community's plea has ended. They waited expectantly for the Lord to answer. God's people were confident that his silence would end. They were confident because they had prepared themselves for renewal. We cannot force God's hand. God acts according to his plans. But this psalm reminds us of what we can do: turn to God, show reverence (fear), and pray.

Verses 10–13 envision the answer to the community's prayers. In verse 10, four core attributes of God appear as if they are partners in a relationship: loyal, committed love links with faithfulness; righteousness and peace greet one another with a kiss. God's people can count on their future because of who God is at his core. Imagine the ideal leader, who is predictably loving and compassionate and who works for justice and wholeness for all. If this is what you desire, the good news is that the God of the Bible defines these ideals. Verse 11 changes the image from relationships to the expanse of creation. Faithfulness connects with righteousness just as the earth reaches up to meet the sky. What does this mean for God's people? In a word, it means that the future will be good because God will act to restore the fortunes of his people. Verse 13 pictures God on the move, bringing to pass righteousness and, by implication, love, faithfulness, and peace too. God's good future is coming. Be ready.

1. How does Psalm 85 offer a message of hope for us during difficult and spiritually challenging seasons?

2. What actions does Psalm 85 encourage God's people to take during times of waiting on God?

FIVE

Psalm 87

Psalm 87 (ESV) *On the holy mount stands the city he founded; [2]the LORD loves the gates of Zion more than all the dwelling places of Jacob. [3]Glorious things of you are spoken, O city of God. Selah*

[4]Among those who know me I mention Rahab and Babylon; behold, Philistia and Tyre, with Cush—"This one was born there," they say. [5]And of Zion it shall be said, "This one and that one were born in her"; for the Most High himself will establish her. [6]The LORD records as he registers the peoples, "This one was born there." Selah [7]Singers and dancers alike say, "All my springs are in you."

Key Observation. Zion is the hope of all people, and God's people witness to this reality.

Understanding the Word. Psalm 87 closes out our week with a psalm celebrating Zion. As we saw with Psalms 46–48, songs of Zion remind God's people of his rule over his kingdom. In the Old Testament, God's reign centers on Zion, the mountain where the temple stood in Jerusalem. Psalm 87 offers a positive assessment of the nations. We've seen the nations as threats in previous psalms, but in Psalm 87, they become children of Zion (v. 5). This psalm is important for God's people because it keeps his mission in the forefront of worship. As we've emphasized through our reading of the Psalms, God's people exist to serve as agents of his blessing to the nations. This remains our calling as followers of Jesus (see Matthew 28:18–20; Ephesians 2:8–10; 1 Peter 2:9–10).

Verses 1–3 offer praise to Zion as God's city. Zion stands "on the holy mount" (v. 1). As we learned in Psalm 48, the ancients believed that gods reigned from holy mountains. Thus the mountains of Sinai (e.g., Exodus 19–25) and Zion served critical roles in the Old Testament. God gave the law to Moses at Sinai. Zion became the mountain in Israel where God established his temple. Of course, God's people did not believe that God was confined to either Zion or the temple (see 1 Kings 8:27). Rather, Zion was a powerful symbol of God's presence, power, and rule. Verse 2 uses the language of love to emphasize God's commitment to and choice of Zion as the center of God's reign. Verse 3 celebrates Zion. In verse 7, we will find an example of the "glorious things" (v. 3) spoken about Zion.

Verses 4–6 are good news for all people. Verse 4 includes a list of nations, including some hostile to Israel (all but Tyre and Cush, which some scholars translate as Ethiopia and the ESV suggests may be Nubia, or today's southern Egypt and northern Sudan). "Rahab" is a reference to Egypt. These nations know the Lord. Verses 5–6 use the same language of birth to describe the nations and Israel. In other words, this psalm has an inclusive view of God's final salvation. God is not against the nations, but for them. God desires all to come to know him.

Verse 7 ends the psalm in celebration. Zion is a source of life-giving waters (see Ezekiel 47; cf. Psalm 46:4). This river of life is for the world.

In the New Testament, the temple as the center of God's reigning presence shifts. God's people, through the indwelling of the Holy Spirit, become temples that bear the presence of God into the world. This is the mission of the church—to reflect God's character in/to/for the world. In other words, through the Spirit, followers of Jesus move into the world with the gospel rather than waiting for the world to come to a central location, like a physical temple. We live as visible images of the invisible God by manifesting God's character.

1. What role does Zion play in the faith of God's people? How does this shift in the New Testament?
2. What does Psalm 87 teach us about the hope of the nations, including nations who have persecuted God's people?

WEEK SEVEN

GATHERING DISCUSSION OUTLINE

A. Open session in prayer.

B. View video for this week's reading.

C. What general impressions and thoughts do you have after considering the video and reading the daily writings on these Scriptures? What, specifically, did this week's psalms teach you about faith, life, and prayer?

D. Discuss selected questions from the daily readings. Always invite class members to share key insights or to raise questions that they found to be the most meaningful.

1. **KEY OBSERVATION (PSALM 82):** The true mark of faithfulness is the practice of justice and mercy toward the marginalized.

   DISCUSSION QUESTION: What are the marks of a just world? As God's people, how can we participate in its making?

2. **KEY OBSERVATION (PSALM 83):** When threatened by enemies, God's people pray for protection, but also for the salvation of those opposing them.

   DISCUSSION QUESTION: How does Psalm 83 teach God's people to pray when threatened by enemies?

3. **KEY OBSERVATION (PSALM 84):** The memory and practice of God's presence fuels a meaningful and happy life.

DISCUSSION QUESTION: How does the psalmist's enthusiasm about God's presence help you understand the happy life?

4. **KEY OBSERVATION (PSALM 85):** When in need of restoration, turn with reverence and prayer to the God of love, mercy, faithfulness, and compassion.

   DISCUSSION QUESTION: How does Psalm 85 offer a message of hope for us during difficult and spiritually challenging seasons?

5. **KEY OBSERVATION (PSALM 87):** Zion is the hope of all people, and God's people witness to this reality.

   DISCUSSION QUESTION: What does Psalm 87 teach us about the hope of the nations, including nations who have persecuted God's people?

E. Close session with prayer.

WEEK EIGHT

Book III: The Desperation and Destiny of God's People

ONE

Psalm 88:1–5

Psalm 88:1–5 (ESV) *O Lord, God of my salvation, I cry out day and night before you.* [2]*Let my prayer come before you; incline your ear to my cry!*

[3]*For my soul is full of troubles, and my life draws near to Sheol.* [4]*I am counted among those who go down to the pit; I am a man who has no strength,* [5]*like one set loose among the dead, like the slain that lie in the grave, like those whom you remember no more, for they are cut off from your hand.*

Key Observation. Desperate laments arise out of a deep faith in the Lord, who invites us to pray openly and honestly.

Understanding the Word. Psalms 88 and 89 bring Book III of the Psalter to a conclusion in anguished lament. In Psalm 88 an individual struggled with God's absence. Psalm 89 reflects on God's absence from a national perspective. These dark psalms will help us in times of suffering and instruct us to serve others in need. The book of Psalms serves as the prayer book for our journey through life as God's missional people. As we've seen in our reading of Books II–III, people of faith are not immune from challenges. God understands this reality. Life is not easy. These two psalms give us words to pray when our foundations are shaken and our easy answers sound empty. Don't fear feelings that overwhelm during such times or think that we must hide them from God. As these two psalms demonstrate, God is ready to hear our prayers because the God who, in Jesus, died for all suffering, sin, and injustice, is risen, present, and in the process of making all things new.

Psalm 88 is the most forlorn of all the laments. The psalmist was in true anguish. The psalmist's sense of forsakenness and rejection was extreme. Yet his faith and hope in the Lord remained. The psalmist was desperate for God to act.

The psalm opens with the psalmist engaging the Lord as the "God of my salvation." This is a critical starting point that roots what otherwise is a difficult psalm within the *relationship* between the psalmist and the Lord. Who is the Lord to the psalmist? The Lord is the *God of my salvation*. There was a personal trust present despite the psalmist's circumstances. This is the heart of lament. The psalmist recognized the identity and character of the Lord as the God who saves, past, present, and future. This reality is unchanging even if the psalmist had not received relief from his affliction.

In verses 1b–2, the psalmist moved from confession of faith in God to taking action by praying and pleading for relief. This was no morning or evening prayer. This was ongoing, continuous, one-way communication with God. The psalmist was desperate.

Verses 3–5 sketch out the psalmist's plight in a general yet serious way. The psalmist felt as though he were standing within inches of death's door. He confessed a sense of being overwhelmed, weak, and lonely.

As you read through the words of this psalm today and tomorrow, see the psalmist's circumstances and actions and hear his underlying assumptions:

- The psalmist confessed authentic faith and trust in the Lord as the "God of my salvation."
- The psalmist was suffering greatly.
- The psalmist prayed fervently for God to act, but there was no immediate answer.
- The psalmist continued to pray with a sense of "I don't get it, Lord. Where are you?"

One of the challenges of Psalm 88 is that there is no apparent answer. As we will see, perhaps this *is* the answer.

1. Reflect on a difficult challenge or crisis that you've personally faced. How did your prayer life change?
2. How can Psalm 88's sad and desperate tone serve as a model for our prayers?

TWO

Psalm 88:6-18

Psalm 88:6–18 (ESV) *You have put me in the depths of the pit, in the regions dark and deep.* [7]*Your wrath lies heavy upon me, and you overwhelm me with all your waves. Selah*

[8]*You have caused my companions to shun me; you have made me a horror to them. I am shut in so that I cannot escape;* [9]*my eye grows dim through sorrow. Every day I call upon you, O Lord; I spread out my hands to you.* [10]*Do you work wonders for the dead? Do the departed rise up to praise you? Selah* [11]*Is your steadfast love declared in the grave, or your faithfulness in Abaddon?* [12]*Are your wonders known in the darkness, or your righteousness in the land of forgetfulness?*

[13]*But I, O Lord, cry to you; in the morning my prayer comes before you.* [14]*O Lord, why do you cast my soul away? Why do you hide your face from me?* [15]*Afflicted and close to death from my youth up, I suffer your terrors; I am helpless.* [16]*Your wrath has swept over me; your dreadful assaults destroy me.* [17]*They surround me like a flood all day long; they close in on me together.* [18]*You have caused my beloved and my friend to shun me; my companions have become darkness.*

Key Observation. The power of the gospel is that it is good news available to us even *in the darkest moments of life.*

Understanding the Word. Psalm 88 takes a challenging turn in verse 6. The opening of Psalm 88 expressed the psalmist's trust in the Lord as the "God of my salvation" (1a), his commitment to constant prayer, and his sense of nearness to death. Beginning in verse 6, the psalmist's plight got *real* and challenging. The psalmist blamed God openly for the suffering that he experienced.

Read the words of verses 6–18 again slowly. Allow yourself to feel the psalmist's desperation and pain. This was a prayer to the One whom the psalmist considered both responsible for his current state and his only *hope*.

In verses 6–9a, the psalmist accused the Lord of being the cause of his torment. This sounds jarring to our ears. We tend to affirm that "God is good all the time, and all the time God is good." He certainly is. The psalmist would not dispute this intellectually, but at a felt level, there will be times when suffering is unbearable and God seems indifferent. When God's revealed character does not live up to our experiences, this psalm provides words for us to pray.

At the heart of this lament, the psalmist confessed his desire to maintain relationship and to serve as a witness to the world (vv. 9b–12). The psalmist echoed key parts of God's character: love, faithfulness, acts of wonder, and righteousness. Despite his experience, the psalmist recognized that God is a God of salvation. Yet how will the world learn of the greatness of the Lord if the psalmist died without sharing this news? Thus, the psalmist desired deliverance not merely for his own sake but so that others may know the Lord.

In the psalm's conclusion (vv. 13–18), the psalmist cried out for help and accused the Lord of abandoning him to despair and darkness. Verse 18 ends the psalm with a forlorn declaration of deep isolation. The psalmist was friendless except for the presence of darkness.

Psalm 88 is a psalm for those dark times in life when we lie awake on our beds with minds that will not stop. It is a psalm for seasons when we experience one loss after another. It is a psalm that reminds us that life and faith do not always have fairy-tale endings. We long for tidiness and a world where easy answers abound, but life is often more challenging.

Followers of Jesus are not immune to suffering. Each of us can find ourselves in deep pain, suffering from inoperable cancer, the loss of a child, divorce, or as victims of senseless violence, persecution, or extreme poverty. Psalm 88 tells us to pray through insurmountable situations with honesty and with vigor.

We do not know the outcome of life for the psalmist, but we do have his words as a gift for those days and seasons when we face dark nights of the soul. As followers of Jesus, we also have the hope of a God who understands personally our deepest suffering.

1. What does the lack of a happy ending in Psalm 88 say about our life of faith and our prayers?
2. How does Psalm 88 challenge your faith? How does it affirm it?

THREE

Psalm 89:1–4

Psalm 89:1–4 (ESV) *I will sing of the steadfast love of the LORD, forever; with my mouth I will make known your faithfulness to all generations. [2]For I said, "Steadfast love will be built up forever; in the heavens you will establish your faithfulness." [3]You have said, "I have made a covenant with my chosen one; I have sworn to David my servant: [4]'I will establish your offspring forever, and build your throne for all generations.'" Selah*

Key Observation. Love and faithfulness are the defining center of God's character and the foundation for our relationship with him.

Understanding the Word. If Psalm 88 offers a prayer for times of intense suffering and abandonment, Psalm 89 raises the stakes to the level of a national catastrophe. Psalm 89 reflects on the failure of God's promises to David to keep God's people safe from harm.

The psalmist opened with a vow declaring his intention to proclaim the Lord's love and faithfulness to all generations (v. 1). The pairing of love and faithfulness occurs throughout the Old Testament. A loyal and predictable love fills the internal character of the Lord. These attributes describe God's loving commitment to his promises to his people. God demonstrated this love in the Old Testament by keeping his promises to Israel's ancestors (Abraham, Isaac, and Jacob), delivering his people from slavery in Egypt, giving his people the Law at Sinai, gifting the land of Canaan to his people, establishing Jerusalem as the central place of worship, and raising up David and his descendants to rule forever over God's kingdom. The psalmist focused on the last of these acts. Verse 2 reinforces the power of the psalmist's praise. The psalmist would lift up God's love and faithfulness forever *because* they are the rock-solid foundation for life.

The psalmist's way of life *assumed* that God is unchanging and true. As we will see, the struggle occurs when God's character and will appear to have changed in midstream. This leads to a faith crisis.

Verses 3–4 turn from a broad view of God's faithful love to a specific application of it in history. The psalmist remembered the Lord's promises to David (see 2 Samuel 7:11–16). God promised David that his family would rule over God's kingdom forever. This unconditional promise is known as the Davidic covenant. The Lord chose David and his descendants to serve as the human agents through whom God would expand his kingdom of peace to the world. This promise to David was rock-solid because the Lord spoke it.

The next two sections of Psalm 89 expand further on the grounding and details of the Lord's promise to David. In verses 5–18, the psalmist praised God for his mighty wonders. He was not thinking about God's action on behalf of Israel, but rather, about God's power as Creator and Sustainer of the universe. In the psalmist's mind, the Lord is incomparable (vv. 6–8). No other so-called god or part of creation is worthy of being mentioned in the same sentence as the Lord. Since this is true, God's promises, love, and faithfulness are truly eternal.

Then verses 19–37 review God's powerful guidance and protection of David. Through David, God defeats all the enemies and forces that threaten God's people. In fact, Israel's future is secure because God will be faithful to David no matter what.

If Psalm 89 concluded here, all would be well and this would be a beloved psalm of praise. But as we will see tomorrow, Psalm 89 takes a dramatic shift.

1. Examine your core beliefs about God and the world. Briefly describe how they serve as a foundation for your faith.

2. Which of God's characteristics do you find yourself most frequently praising?

FOUR

Psalm 89:38–52

Psalm 89:38–52 *But you have rejected, you have spurned, you have been very angry with your anointed one.* [39]*You have renounced the covenant with your servant and have defiled his crown in the dust.* [40]*You have broken through all his walls and reduced his strongholds to ruins.* [41]*All who pass by have plundered him; he has become the scorn of his neighbors.* [42]*You have exalted the right hand of his foes; you have made all his enemies rejoice.* [43]*Indeed, you have turned back the edge of his sword and have not supported him in battle.* [44]*You have put an end to his splendor and cast his throne to the ground.* [45]*You have cut short the days of his youth; you have covered him with a mantle of shame.*

[46]*How long, LORD? Will you hide yourself forever? How long will your wrath burn like fire?* [47]*Remember how fleeting is my life. For what futility you have created all humanity!* [48]*Who can live and not see death, or who can escape the power of the grave?* [49]*Lord, where is your former great love, which in your faithfulness you swore to David?* [50]*Remember, Lord, how your servant has been mocked, how I bear in my heart the taunts of all the nations,* [51]*the taunts with which your enemies, LORD, have mocked, with which they have mocked every step of your anointed one.*

[52]*Praise be to the LORD forever! Amen and Amen.*

Key Observation. Even when all appears lost, God's people resolutely stand on his promises to bring salvation and renewal.

Understanding the Word. Psalm 89 opens with a general praise of the Lord for God's faithful love and for his committed promises to King David (vv. 1–4). In verses 5–37, the psalmist grounded the praise in the wonders of God as Creator and Sustainer and for God's actions through David. Then in verse 38, Psalm 89 takes a dramatic turn when the psalmist reveals his plight. The psalmist was not writing from safety. He was writing post-catastrophe from a position of oppression. Psalm 89 assumes the destruction of Jerusalem, including its temple and the end of Davidic rule. This happened at the hand of Babylon in 587 BC. Psalm 89 shifts from a bold and daring praise hymn to a challenging lament for God to renew his people, kingdom, and king.

Verses 38–45 indicate that a reversal of fortune has happened. Rather than enjoying the security and victories detailed in verses 5–37, the psalmist rehearsed chaos and defeat. David stood rejected rather than chosen. The eternal covenant with David appeared to have been a false promise. Jerusalem was laid waste (v. 40). All who gazed upon David and Jerusalem picked through the leftovers and looked on it with shame (v. 41). God's enemies had triumphed (v. 42). The reign of David and his descendants was at an end (vv. 43–45). Rather than in honor and glory, God's people lived in shame.

The significance of this national catastrophe for understanding the Old Testament cannot be overemphasized. The defeat to Babylon and the experience of exile seared pain into the consciousness of God's people. They feared that God's promises had failed.

Yet the closing verses of Psalm 89 (vv. 46–52) suggest a different truth. God's people did not lose faith and hope in the Lord. They faced a season of pain, but they steadfastly trusted that their God would again act. In fact, the tone of Psalm 89's closing calls for action demonstrate resolute confidence in God's justice and love. Notice how verses 46–48 and 49–51 follow a repeating pattern of petition to God. Both of these petitions address the problem of God's perceived absence and inactivity. The psalmist, who spoke as the Davidic king, reminded God of the shortness of life and shame felt by God's people in the absence of his saving love and activity. Verse 51 lifts up the plight faced specifically by God's anointed king. This is a prayer for God to again shine his favor on the messiah in order to restore God's people.

This remains the longing of all God's people whenever they find themselves in times of distress. Psalm 89 is a prayer for help when the world is turned upside down. Yet it is also a prayer that is confident in the Lord and trusts that God will act. Verse 52 ends Psalm 89 and Book III with a concluding affirmation and burst of praise.

1. How does Psalm 89 teach God's people to pray when their foundation has been rocked with uncertainty?
2. How was the psalmist able to remain hopeful despite his accusation that God's promises had failed?

FIVE
Concluding Reflections

Key Observation. Psalms 88–89 provide rich reflection on suffering and the life of faith.

Understanding the Word. You may be surprised that Book III ends with Psalms 88–89. Our culture loves happy endings, but at this point in the journey, God's people found themselves in the chaos of the storm. Psalm 88 reminds us that there will be personal crises that cut deep. Psalm 89 testifies to dark days in which all God's people struggle in the face of catastrophic change.

What can we take away from our study of Books II and III of the Psalms in general and the concluding Psalms 88–89 in particular?

(1) There will be times of winter and struggle. God's people exist to live missionally among the nations by testifying to God's goodness and love. This calling often stands at odds with the culture. This may bring suffering. Also, God's people may turn away from the Lord, and with this comes self-inflicted pain and struggle. Regardless of the cause, the Psalms do not sugarcoat the life of faith. There will be valleys along the journey.

(2) God is still active and present. Throughout our study, we've encountered the deep trust of God's people in his activity and presence. Psalms 88–89 testify to the pain and disappointment of God's people, but even in personal and national tragedy, the psalmists remained resolute that the Lord is the only secure source of hope and salvation. They anticipated God's answering their prayers.

(3) There remains a beautiful future. History is moving toward love, reconciliation, peace, justice, mercy, and beauty. This is the promise of Scripture. Through the life, death, and resurrection of Jesus Christ, God is making all things new (see 2 Corinthians 5:17; Revelation 21:5). The Psalter began in the security of Scripture and God's reign (see Psalms 1–2) and it will end in a climax of praise (see Psalms 146–150). This future remains secure because God can be trusted.

(4) Return to your roots: gratitude, trust, and faithfulness. *The Psalms—Part III* will begin with Psalm 90 and cover Books IV and V. Psalm 90 is attributed to Moses. This is significant. It points to the way through chaos by calling God's people to return to the teachings of Moses. How do we live in the midst of suffering? We remember the past goodness of God and give thanks. We continue to trust God that our future remains in his good hands. We read Scripture as our guide. Then we act faithfully and walk moment by moment in love for God and neighbor regardless of present circumstances. This is the road modeled by our forerunners in the faith (see Hebrews 12:1–3).

(5) Disappointment can serve as a proving ground for growing into the people whom God created us to be. The good news is that God will make all things new. The gospel shows us that resurrection stands on the other side of crucifixion. Dawn follows the blackness of night. The psalms will follow a similar pattern. The Psalter ends with all creation praising God (see Psalms 146–150). Growing through the chaos of life and walking faithfully prepares us to participate unabashedly in the glorious future that awaits us in Christ (see Romans 8:18–30).

1. How do Psalms 88–89 provide us with resources for responding to times of struggle?
2. What does the lack of a happy ending to Book III teach us about the life and journey of faith?

WEEK EIGHT

GATHERING DISCUSSION OUTLINE

A. Open session in prayer.

B. View video for this week's reading.

C. What general impressions and thoughts do you have after considering the video and reading the daily writings on these Scriptures? What, specifically, did this week's psalms teach you about faith, life, and prayer?

D. Discuss selected questions from the daily readings. Always invite class members to share key insights or to raise questions that they found to be the most meaningful.

1. **KEY OBSERVATION (PSALM 88:1–5):** Desperate laments arise out of a deep faith in the Lord, who invites us to pray openly and honestly.

   DISCUSSION QUESTION: Reflect on a difficult challenge or crisis that you've personally faced. How did your prayer life change?

2. **KEY OBSERVATION (PSALM 88:6–18):** The power of the gospel is that it is good news available to us even *in the darkest moments of life.*

   DISCUSSION QUESTION: What does the lack of a happy ending in Psalm 88 say about our life of faith and our prayers?

3. **KEY OBSERVATION (PSALM 89:1–4):** Love and faithfulness are the defining center of God's character and the foundation for our relationship with him.

DISCUSSION QUESTION: Examine your core beliefs about God and the world. Briefly describe how they serve as a foundation for your faith.

4. **KEY OBSERVATION (PSALM 89:38–52):** Even when all appears lost, God's people resolutely stand on his promises to bring salvation and renewal.

   DISCUSSION QUESTION: How does Psalm 89 teach God's people to pray when their foundation has been rocked with uncertainty?

5. **KEY OBSERVATION:** Psalms 88–89 provide rich reflection on suffering and the life of faith.

   DISCUSSION QUESTION: How do Psalms 88–89 provide us with resources for responding to times of struggle? What does the lack of a happy ending to Book III teach us about the life and journey of faith?

E. Close session with prayer.

www.ingramcontent.com/pod-product-compliance
Ingram Content Group UK Ltd.
Pitfield, Milton Keynes, MK11 3LW, UK
UKHW021401070726
13610UKWH00012B/66

9 781628 244373